RTI
Assessment
Essentials
for
Struggling
Learners

JOHN J. HOOVER

CORWIN
A SAGE Company

For information:

Corwin
A SAGE Company
2455 Teller Road
Thousand Oaks, California 91320
(800) 233-9936
Fax: (800) 417-2466
www.corwinpress.com

SAGE Ltd.
1 Oliver's Yard
55 City Road
London EC1Y 1SP
United Kingdom

SAGE India Pvt. Ltd.
B 1/I 1 Mohan Cooperative
   Industrial Area
Mathura Road, New Delhi
India 110 044

SAGE Asia-Pacific Pte. Ltd.
33 Pekin Street #02-01
Far East Square
Singapore 048763

Printed in the United States of America.

Library of Congress Cataloging-in-Publication Data

Hoover, John J.
RTI assessment essentials for struggling learners/John J. Hoover.
     p. cm.
Includes bibliographical references and index.
ISBN 978-1-4129-6953-6 (cloth)
ISBN 978-1-4129-6954-3 (pbk.)
   1. Remedial teaching. 2. Slow learning children—Rating of. I. Title.

LB1029.R4H66 2009
372.48—dc22   2008044778

This book is printed on acid-free paper.

09   10   11   12   13   10   9   8   7   6   5   4   3   2   1

Acquisitions Editor:	David Chao
Editorial Assistant:	Mary Dang and Brynn Saito
Production Editor:	Eric Garner
Copy Editor:	Gretchen Treadwell
Typesetter:	C&M Digitals (P) Ltd.
Proofreader:	Susan Schon
Indexer:	Jean Casalegno
Cover Designer:	Michael Dubowe

Contents

List of Forms

Note: All forms are designed as informal guides to assist educators in addressing important topics, issues, and practices essential to the area to which each form relates. Forms were developed from literature sources cited in the book as well as the author's educational experiences over the past several decades. All forms were field reviewed for accuracy and clarity of content by several professionals.

Preface

Assessment Perspective in Today's Instructional Environments

Not since the passage of PL 94–142 in the mid-1970s has our educational system witnessed such a national shift in teaching and learning to meet the needs of at-risk and struggling learners as we have in response to intervention (RTI). This shift is characterized by refocusing our assessment efforts from determining "intrinsic deficits" to "quality and effectiveness" of instruction. For decades, our approach to meeting the needs of struggling learners was one of looking for intrinsic disorders to diagnose disabilities through a model that generally waited until the learner was significantly behind in academic or social-emotional development; specialized instruction (i.e., special education) then became the preferred option to best address the exhibited needs. Assessment practices over time focused on comparing students to students using standardized, norm referenced devices on a large-scale basis throughout our school systems.

For significant numbers of students who were struggling with learning, the assessment and associated educational model adhered to over the past few decades was one of refer, test, and place relative to special education. Less assessment emphasis was placed on the quality of instruction, rigorousness of implemented interventions, connection between that which was taught to that which was assessed, or relationships between student progress and teacher effectiveness. In our efforts to identify "deficits" within the learner to best understand student needs, we oftentimes neglected to evaluate the quality of instruction, effectiveness of the instruction, or to what extent students were actually learning what they were directly taught.

While inferences may have been made about these "instructional" variables, the needs of struggling learners were primarily grounded in perceived identified deficits within the student. In addition, while concerns with this type of deficit approach and model have existed for years, school systems continued to implement these practices perpetuating what has become to be known as the "wait to fail" model, where educational assistance and supplemental support are only provided after a period of significant failures occurred over extended periods of time. This "wait to fail" model has been structured in such a way that many learners who clearly show signs of struggling in school are provided less assistance early in the process of efforts to prevent potential problems from becoming more significant.

However, with the passage of No Child Left Behind (NCLB) in 2001 and the reauthorization of Individuals with Disabilities Education Act (IDEA) in 2004, significant changes resulted in ways of thinking about why students struggle in school and how their needs should be best identified and subsequently addressed. Factors such as research-based curriculum, evidence-based interventions, multi-tiered instruction, highly qualified teachers, and response to intervention began to quickly sweep through our educational system. From a national perspective, Hoover, Baca, Love, and Saenz (2008) found that almost every state in the United States has or is planning to implement some form of multi-tiered response to intervention in their schools. The national shift to multi-tiered, research-based instruction is significant to assessment of struggling learners for a variety of reasons including the following:

1. Initial assessment focuses on quality of instruction and not intrinsic deficits.

2. Struggling learners are identified early in their schooling through structured screening.

3. The progress of struggling learners is assessed and monitored on a frequent, periodic basis.

4. Quick, easy to implement assessments are conducted at regular intervals using standardized procedures and valid measures.

5. Assessment data reflecting actual student progress provide the foundation for making instructional decisions.

6. Should special education be considered necessary, it will be determined only after high-quality instruction by highly qualified teachers has been implemented and corroborated.

As can be seen, the above items reflect a significant departure from the previous "wait to fail" model by focusing initially on quality of instruction, frequent assessments, charted data points to illustrate progress (or lack thereof), as well as decisions based on the direct connections between that which is taught and that which is assessed. An emphasis on three types of assessments is included in this new model: universal screening, progress monitoring, and diagnostic. Universal screening identifies struggling learners early in school, progress monitoring determines student progress over time, and diagnostic pinpoints and clarifies individual needs and suspected disabilities. *The current emphasis in our educational system is to provide multi-tiered or layered instruction that increases in intensity and duration based on assessed student progress directly resulting from classroom instruction.*

In regards to diagnostic assessment, it is important to bear in mind that this type of assessment, as we have seen its implementation over the past few decades, is still an important component of multi-tiered instruction. However, diagnosing suspected disabilities and individual learning needs where specialized instruction may be necessary occurs after: (1) high-quality instruction in the general class curriculum has been implemented and corroborated, (2) student is provided supplemental support to assist with learning the general class curriculum, (3) progress made toward achievement is assessed at regular intervals, (4) instruction is adjusted based on progress-monitoring results, and (5) attempts to implement evidence-based instruction increasing in intensity and duration are clearly documented along with student response to that instruction. Therefore, in regards to assessment within this structure, use of effective, relevant, and evidence-based devices and practices must be implemented with the highest integrity if multi-tiered response to intervention is to succeed with all learners.

Acknowledgments

Over the past three decades, I have had the privilege of working with many educators in several different states who strive to complete assessments for struggling learners with the utmost integrity. I wish to acknowledge the service and work of all the educators with whom I have had and continue to have the privilege of knowing and working with over the years. The demands associated with conducting effective and relevant assessment continues to challenge us all, particularly as accountability for student progress increases. The dedication of these educators is highly appreciated as we move into a multi-tiered response to intervention framework for conducting quality assessment. I wish to also acknowledge the field reviewers of this book:

Kathy Amacher
Special Education Teacher
Franklin Middle School
Wheaton, IL

Edward J. Drugo
Retired Principal
Greater Latrobe School District
Greensburg, PA

Phyllis N. Levert
College Teacher; School Administrator
Clark Atlanta University; Georgia School Districts
Atlanta, GA

In addition, I wish to thank the educators who reviewed and have used the different forms in this book and provided feedback concerning their development and revisions, especially Ms. Amy Boele, doctoral student at the University of Colorado at Boulder. The comments and suggestions from each of these professionals improved the quality of this book and added valuable content to best assist educators in the assessment of struggling learners in today's schools.

About the Author

John J. Hoover is a former K–12 special education teacher for students with learning disabilities and emotional/behavior disorders in several states in the Midwest, West, and Southwest. He has worked as an educational supervisor, trainer, and evaluator in the area of multicultural special education for over three decades. He earned a BA in Elementary and Special Education (Mental Retardation), an MA in Learning Disabilities and Emotional Disorders with an emphasis in Reading, and a PhD in Curriculum specializing in Special Education. He has over sixty publications including his new book—*Differentiating Learning Differences From Disabilities: Meeting Diverse Needs Through Multi-Tiered Response to Intervention* (Allyn & Bacon, 2009) and recent books coauthored/coedited—*Methods for Teaching Culturally and Linguistically Diverse Exceptional Learners* (Pearson Merrill, 2008); *Why Do English Language Learners Struggle With Reading?* (Corwin Press, 2008); *Curriculum Adaptations for Students With Learning and Behavior Problems: Differentiating Instruction to Meet Diverse Needs* (Pro-Ed, 2005); and *Teaching Study Skills to Students With Learning Problems* (Pro-Ed, 2007). His forthcoming tests include the *Early Literacy Measure* (Pro-Ed) and the *Behavior Skills Rating System* (Pro-Ed). He is currently a Senior Research Associate and adjunct faculty in the School of Education at the University of Colorado, Boulder.

Introduction

The education of struggling learners within a multi-tiered response to intervention model has been initiated in most school systems nationwide. To this end, state departments of education, districts/schools as well as personal efforts have led to increased educator knowledge and skills associated with a multi-tiered instructional framework. While a variety of educational aspects (e.g., evidence-based, data-driven decisions, screening, etc.) are addressed in the transition to multi-tiered response to intervention, the effective implementation of the overall assessment process is fundamental to ensuring its success. Given the significance of different levels and frequencies of gathering assessment data in multi-tiered response to intervention, it is imperative that all concerned possess sufficient grounding in assessment to best facilitate its use for educating all learners in today's classrooms.

This practical book provides educators a comprehensive overview of essential elements necessary for completing assessment for at-risk and struggling learners educated within multi-tiered response to intervention models. *RTI Assessment Essentials for Struggling Learners* includes detailed coverage of the three primary assessment types within multi-tiered instruction: (1) universal screening, (2) ongoing progress monitoring, and (3) diagnostic assessment for special education. Assessment strategies and decision-making processes are addressed throughout this book. This includes consideration of the fact that some students educated within a multi-tiered instructional model may eventually be referred and evaluated for possible special education eligibility and placement, emphasizing the significance of all three levels of assessment for struggling learners in today's schools.

This book focuses primarily on one of the most fundamental issues within multi-tiered response to intervention; that is, the assessment processes within which the most important decisions about struggling learners are made. The book includes nine chapters divided into three major parts: Foundation, Implementation, and Decision Making. Part I includes three chapters that establish the foundation for assessment in multi-tiered response to intervention including an overview of RTI, ecological assessment framework within RTI, and the assessment continuum along which universal screening, ongoing progress monitoring, and diagnostic assessment occur. Part II includes three chapters that address the important topics of assessment fidelity, assessment devices and assessment practices as well as the role of RTI in the overall special education diagnostic eligibility assessment process. Part III also includes three chapters that discuss the topics of decision making, meeting RTI needs of culturally and linguistically diverse learners struggling in school, as well as specific attention to some of the issues that continue to challenge educators as we move forward with multi-tiered assessment and instruction. Throughout the chapters, various tables and figures are presented to facilitate practical application of the assessment topics covered. In addition, there are seventeen reproducible forms that contain guides or checklists for direct use within the multi-tiered response to intervention assessment process.

Each chapter also contains a Personal Perspective section in which I share personal experiences relative to the chapter's main topic. All chapters begin with an overview of the topic's significance to contemporary assessment, key topics, and learner outcomes and end with suggested activities to apply the learner outcomes addressed in the chapter. The Appendix contains an overview PowerPoint/overhead slide presentation that professional developers may use in training educators in the assessment essentials discussed in this book.

RTI Assessment Essentials for Struggling Learners is written for all practitioners directly involved in the implementation of multi-tiered response to intervention. It is appropriate for all educators since comprehensive assessment data must be gathered, analyzed, charted, and used to make ongoing instructional and/or eligibility decisions within each tier of instruction in the RTI process. This includes assessment associated with general class instruction, supplemental or intensive interventions, as well as eligibility decision making for possible special education. In addition to being a text for professional development on assessment within multi-tiered RTI, this book will serve as a valuable supplemental text in college/university undergraduate and graduate courses on diagnostic and authentic assessment of struggling learners and those at risk. It is my hope that the contents of this book assist educators to form or expand their expertise of assessment to more fairly screen, monitor, or diagnose progress and needs of struggling learners in valid and reliable ways as mandated by multi-tiered response to intervention models.

—JJH

PART I

Foundations of Assessment in Multi-Tiered RTI

The fundamental shift seen in today's schools to meet the needs of struggling learners is one of moving away from the more traditional assessment to identify deficits within the child to identifying the most appropriate form of instruction within which the learner best responds. This complex system includes two interrelated elements: (1) structure and components necessary for providing effective instruction, and (2) process for determining the extent to which the instruction is effective in meeting learner needs. To best understand these two elements, Part I includes three chapters that address the topics of multi-tiered instruction, an ecological framework for providing and assessing instruction as well as the general continuum of assessment practices, and procedures and decision making. An understanding of these important features provides the foundation for best understanding and implementing assessment within multi-tiered response to intervention models.

Part I Chapters

1. Overview of Multi-Tiered Response to Intervention for Struggling Learners

2. Assessment Continuum in Multi-Tiered Response to Intervention

3. Ecological Framework Within Multi-Tiered Response to Intervention

1

Overview of Multi-Tiered Response to Intervention for Struggling Learners

SIGNIFICANCE TO CONTEMPORARY ASSESSMENT

The education of struggling learners and those at risk in learning in today's classrooms is framed within the practice of multi-tiered response to intervention (RTI). This framework requires the implementation of research-based instructional and assessment practices grounded in evidence that reflects effectiveness for intended purposes. Fundamental to multi-tiered RTI is the implementation of layers or levels of instruction that become more intensive to meet student needs. An understanding of the process of multi-tiered learning and the associated student responses to the interventions implemented is critical to providing effective assessment to all learners in today's classrooms. This includes being knowledgeable of the concept of data-driven decision making as well as the structure for selecting and implementing various levels of instruction and assessment in today's schools and classrooms.

Note: The terms "evidence-based" and "research-based" refer to a similar concept that reflects practices/curricula that have been demonstrated to be effective for specified purposes with defined populations based on research. These two terms are used interchangeably throughout this book.

CHAPTER OVERVIEW

Chapter 1 provides discussion of the primary components embedded within multi-tiered response to intervention models. Readers are provided an overview of the structure and important aspects found in multi-tiered instructional programming necessary to successfully implement RTI to learners at risk and those who struggle in school. Basic assessment processes and components found within multi-tiered response to intervention are also introduced.

Key Topics Addressed in Chapter

✦ Multi-Tiered Instruction

✦ Response to Intervention (RTI)

✦ Evidence-Based Learning and Assessment

✦ Problem-Solving Models

LEARNER OUTCOMES

Upon completion of Chapter 1, readers will

- know and understand the basics associated with multi-tiered RTI
- be able to more effectively implement multi-tiered instruction and assessment
- become familiar with various models for making multi-tiered instructional and assessment decisions
- be able to evaluate their schools' implementation of multi-tiered RTI model

Note: Regarding the use of terms referring to "assessment/problem-solving teams," different schools refer to their assessment decision-making teams in various ways and these are used interchangeably throughout this book. This includes terms such as assessment team, child-study team, teacher-assistance teams, RTI team, problem-solving team or similar terms. As used throughout this book, these terms refer to the school's team designed to make assessment and instructional decisions for struggling and at-risk learners.

PERSONAL PERSPECTIVE

Since multi-tiered response to intervention has become a focal point in today's schools, some of my efforts in this area have included providing assistance to educators in various schools and school systems as they transition into this important educational structure. This includes schools in urban and rural locations and both small and large school systems. I have found that educators are making tremendous strides in understanding multi-tiered RTI, including preparing themselves for this new framework for meeting the needs of struggling learners.

(Continued)

> (Continued)
>
> Some of the positives that I have observed or participated in are: (1) district or state-wide training, (2) development of multi-tiered RTI school-based teams, (3) professional development, and (4) collaborative efforts among different educators. These and similar efforts have assisted many educators to begin the process of moving into a multi-tiered framework.
>
> However, along with these types of positive, proactive efforts I have also observed some potential problem areas within multi-tiered instruction that need to be rectified if this structure is to be successful for all learners. These include: (1) lack of in-depth understanding of evidence-based interventions, (2) roles associated with the required assessment practices, (3) misinterpreting that all students must progress through tiered instruction in exactly the same manner, (4) lack of clarity with how "rate of progress" relates to response to intervention decisions, and (5) new roles that must be assumed by general and special educators in the overall multi-tiered RTI decision-making process. My message to those with whom I have worked is to be certain to understand the underlying principles and practices of response to intervention as discussed in Chapter 1 and involve all school staff in development/implementation of RTI.

INTRODUCTION

Effective education for students who struggle with learning has reached a critical time in today's schools given the increase in mandated curricula and statewide assessments. One result of the increased numbers of students placed into special education is the greater emphasis on prevention and intervention of learning problems sooner rather than later once struggling learners have been identified. The most current framework that many school districts nationwide are adopting is referred to as multi-tiered response to intervention. This educational practice has two interrelated aspects: (1) multi-tiered instructional programming and (2) procedures for determining student response to interventions implemented. While educators are not in total agreement with the specifics associated with multi-tiered RTI, the practice shows promise to better meet the needs of struggling learners over the previously used "wait to fail" models of the 70s, 80s and 90s. Multi-tiered response to intervention is a practice that must be understood from at least two interrelated perspectives: (1) levels of instruction, and (2) data-based decision making. Each of these is discussed below. However, we begin with a summary of key terms and practices discussed throughout this book:

Multi-Tiered Instruction. Layers or levels of instruction that increase in duration and intensity as student needs indicate through assessment data.

Implementation With Fidelity. The implementation of research-based instructional interventions and associated assessments in a manner consistent with the way each was tested and researched.

Evidence-Based Interventions. Instructional interventions that contain research data to support their usage with a specified population of learners for defined purposes.

Response to Intervention. Systematic implementation of evidence-based interventions that increase in duration and intensity based on progress-monitoring data demonstrating student response to instruction.

Data-Driven Decision Making. Practice of using progress-monitoring data and rate of progress reflecting student responses to instruction as the primary basis for making instructional and eligibility decisions.

Universal Screening. Practice by which all students are screened (usually three times per year) to determine their level of attainment of district curricular benchmarks for the purpose of identifying struggling learners.

Progress Monitoring. Task of systematically gathering assessment data to determine the extent to which a student responds to evidence-based instruction by monitoring progress on a frequent basis (e.g., monthly, weekly, daily), based on level or tier of instruction provided.

Diagnostic Assessment. Type of specialized assessment by which individual learning needs are diagnosed to make informed decisions concerning potential special education placement and eligibility.

Ecological. Refers to the learner's total environment including community, home, school, and classroom settings.

Ecological Assessment Factors. Implementation of assessment in a way that considers student, school, and home-community factors in the instructional and diagnostic decision-making process.

Difference Versus Disability. Concept by which learning differences are appropriately identified reducing the misinterpretation of cultural and linguistic differences as disabilities.

Culturally Responsive. Ensuring that various diverse cultural values, norms, languages, and preferred educational practices are considered and accommodated in the education of culturally and linguistically diverse learners.

MULTI-TIERED RESPONSE TO INTERVENTION MODEL: LEVELS OF INSTRUCTION

Multi-level instruction is a structure within which different types of instruction are provided to students based on the extent to which they are meeting defined curricular benchmarks and objectives. These types of instruction increase in intensity and duration as students demonstrate the need for more intensive interventions based on progress monitoring reflecting learner response to instruction. Most models of multi-tiered instruction include three levels of intervention; however, some districts and researchers describe four levels of intervention (Klingner & Edwards, 2006). Our discussions will present three levels since this is the most widely used structure in today's schools.

Three-Tiered Instruction

Multi-tiered instruction is typically illustrated in the form of a pyramid as shown by the following illustration.

Figure 1.1   Three-Tiered Instruction

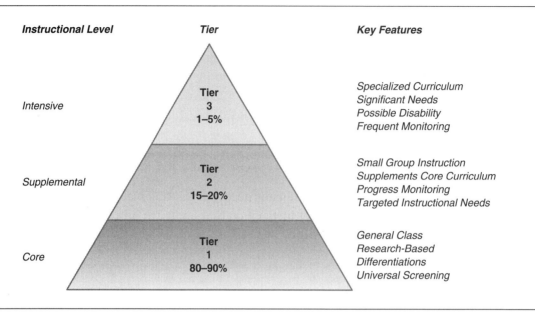

Figure 1.1 and subsequent discussion provides a summary of the levels of interventions in multi-tiered instruction as covered by Bender and Shores (2007), Hoover and Patton (2008), Fuchs and Fuchs (2006), Klingner, Mendez Barletta, and Hoover (2008), Mellard and Johnson (2008), and Vaughn (2003). As illustrated, a multi-tiered instructional framework is characterized by distinct tiers, each associated with a specific level of instruction that reflects key educational needs of learners. It is important to ensure that as tiers of instruction are implemented, they are viewed as dynamic and fluid in nature based upon learner response to the level of instruction provided. In addition, as shown, while the tiered model is depicted as hierarchal, in practice, levels of instruction are associated with the tiers that are interconnected. Understanding the interrelationship among the levels of instruction across the tiers is essential to providing integrated instruction for struggling learners. In effect, tiers and levels of instruction may be viewed interchangeably and as interconnected (see Figure 1.2).

Figure 1.2   Three Instructional Levels and Associated Settings for All Learners

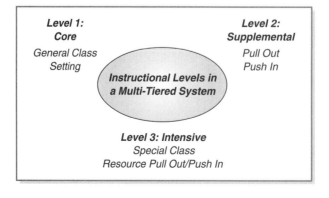

As shown, the three levels of instruction are interconnected, illustrating the all-important concept that a learner may be provided any level of intervention in the most appropriate sequence based on needs and response to classroom instruction. While the expected progression of instruction is sequential from level 1 to 2 to 3, some learners may require a different sequence based on needs. For example, a student with significant needs may be determined to require Tier 3 intensive level of instruction soon after Tier 1 core level of instruction is implemented and progress is assessed. In this example, the student would not be provided Tier 2 level of instruction due to exhibited significant needs, and by doing so would more quickly be provided the most appropriate level of instruction (i.e., Tier 3 without requiring unnecessary Tier 2 level of instruction due to exhibited significant needs). Educators must bear in mind that tiers have associated levels of instruction that are based primarily on student progress, in which flexibility may need to be exercised, rather than strictly adhering to a predetermined and rigid set of parameters, such as requiring that all students must progress through all the levels of instruction in the same sequence regardless of exhibited needs or progress toward achievement of benchmarks (i.e., one size doesn't fit all).

Therefore, multi-tier instruction reflects the *level* of instruction necessary to meet needs. In regards to the location of different levels of instruction, these may occur in the general classroom (e.g., push-in), through pull-out settings, or in a classroom designed for meeting special needs such as a special needs resource classroom. Table 1.1 provides an overview of the assessment components generally associated with each tier of instruction, which are integral to the overall implementation of a multi-tiered model of instruction.

Table 1.1 Assessments Within Three-Tiered Instruction

Tier	Assessment	Expected Outcome	Evidence of Struggling Learner
Core	Universal Screening	Learner successfully meets curricular benchmarks; makes satisfactory rate of progress.	Scores are below expected curricular benchmark standards as indicated by universal screening results; learner fails to make satisfactory rate of progress.
Supplemental	Progress Monitoring	Supplemental supports assist learner to meet curricular objectives/standards found in CORE instruction; student makes satisfactory rate of progress.	Supplemental supports do not assist learner to meet CORE objectives/standards-minimum of two rounds of Tier 2 supplemental supports; learner fails to make adequate rate of progress as evidenced by more frequent progress monitoring.

(Continued)

Table 1.1 (Continued)

Tier	Assessment	Expected Outcome	Evidence of Struggling Learner
Intensive	Progress Monitoring; Diagnostic	Intensive interventions assist learner to make satisfactory rate of progress and/or achieve minimum acceptable level of progress toward achieving curricular benchmarks/ objectives.	Student continues to make inadequate progress toward curricular benchmarks/ objectives after extended period of time receiving intensive instruction designed to meet special needs; special education diagnostic assessment further clarifies special needs along with highly frequent progress monitoring.

As shown, universal screening, progress monitoring, and diagnostic assessment are completed within the overall tiered process. Discussions below provide additional information about each tier of intervention, including reference to associated assessments. (The three assessment types are discussed in greater detail in Chapter 2.)

Tier 1 Core Level of Instruction

The initial level of instruction is implementing research-based curriculum to all learners in the general classroom. To begin the process of identifying struggling learners an assessment process referred to as "universal screening" is completed with all students to assess progress toward curricular benchmarks associated with the research-based curriculum. Universal screening typically includes assessment three times per year (beginning, middle, end) and students not achieving to specified levels (e.g., 25th percentile) are considered at risk in learning. In addition, in some instances, students who do not meet the specified "cut" score who demonstrate a steady and adequate rate of progress are provided more time to meet benchmarks prior to being considered for Tier 2 supplemental instruction.

Rate of response refers to the pace at which a learner progresses. The pace is considered relative to age, grade, and expected growth. Other factors such as experiential background or English language proficiency are also considered when analyzing rate of progress. While subjective to some extent, this concept is critical to ensure that whole groups or classes of students (e.g., English language learners) are not mistakenly considered for a more intensive tier of intervention when additional time within the current level of instruction is most warranted.

Students who are below the "cut" score and who do not demonstrate a sufficient rate of progress are considered struggling learners and are provided supplemental support immediately to assist the student from falling farther behind academically or behaviorally.

Tier 2 Supplemental Level of Instruction

Supplemental instruction is provided to those students who require additional supports to meet the demands and make adequate progress with the Tier 1 core instruction. The Tier 2 level of instruction includes two primary components: (1) targeted supplemental support, and (2) more frequent monitoring of progress. This level of instruction typically includes additional work in a targeted need area (e.g., phonemic awareness, reading fluency) within a more concentrated time frame (e.g., three days per week for thirty minutes a day). This level of small group instruction may occur in the general classroom or in a pull-out setting. The process of Tier 2 instruction requires learners to receive additional support in areas they struggle with in the core instruction. Tier 2 supplemental instruction may be implemented by various educational personnel including the general class teacher, special educator, bilingual/ESL teacher, or reading specialist.

While Tier 1 instruction includes universal screening, usually three times per year, Tier 2 supplemental instruction includes the monitoring of progress on a more frequent basis (e.g., biweekly, weekly). This practice is referred to as ongoing progress monitoring where brief and frequent assessment occurs to more closely monitor student progress. Data from the progress monitoring are charted and used as the foundation for making additional multi-tier instructional decisions. At minimum, two rounds of Tier 2 supplemental instruction should be provided along with charted progress monitoring before a student's progress is determined to be insufficient (Vaughn, 2003). Should learners educated with Tier 2 instruction not make adequate progress, then more intensive Tier 3 interventions are considered necessary.

Tier 3 Intensive Level of Intervention

Students who require Tier 3 interventions have more significant academic and/or behavioral needs as evidenced by falling far below grade-level benchmarks, making inadequate progress with Tier 1 or Tier 2 supplemental instruction. Tier 3 level of instruction provides learners with highly sustained intensive interventions (implemented individually, in pairs, or within small group settings) as well as highly frequent monitoring of progress (e.g., daily, three times per week). Tier 3 interventions may include specialized curriculum and/or highly individualized evidence-based methods such as scripted lessons, direct instruction, analytic teaching, or cognitive strategy usage, along with associated progress monitoring and/or diagnostic assessments. Students who require Tier 3 interventions may be considered for special education (during the later stages of Tier 2 instruction) at which time a formal referral is made and all necessary steps to ensure eligibility must be followed. This may include additional individual diagnostic assessment, classroom observations, interviews, as well as procedures to facilitate culturally responsive assessment.

The implementation of instruction based on levels of needed interventions provides struggling learners with greater opportunities to meet academic and behavioral expectations in a timelier manner and through use of research-based instruction. The frequent monitoring of students' responses to the research-based instruction provides additional safeguards to best assist learners at risk in today's classrooms. As discussed above, multi-tiered response to intervention includes both instructional components as well as assessment components, in which educator teams make decisions concerning levels and types of intervention required.

MULTI-TIERED RESPONSE TO INTERVENTION MODEL: DATA-BASED DECISION MAKING

In addition to emphasizing the implementation of research-based instruction, multi-tiered response to intervention emphasizes the use of data (i.e., diagnostic, universal screening, progress monitoring) as the foundation for making informed instructional decisions. In effect, the level of instruction (Tier 1, 2, or 3) is determined by the data that reflect student response to that instruction. This is referred to as data-based or data-driven decision making and serves as the basis for making decisions reflecting actual instruction implemented in the classroom. This aspect of multi-tier response to intervention reflects a contextualized process of assessing and charting learner performance (as frequently as necessary) to maintain the most current perspective on student needs. According to Brown-Chidsey and Steege (2005), multi-tiered RTI decision making is grounded in the data collected to determine the extent to which learners respond to instruction. In addition, according to Hoover (2006) multi-tiered RTI decision-making processes generate two types of decisions: instructional, which reflects progress-monitoring decisions concerning the most appropriate level of instruction; and diagnostic, which reflects eligibility for special education and further pinpoints student needs.

Data-Based Decision Making

Over the years, multi-tiered response to intervention has grown out of pervasive concerns reflecting two critical aspects in classroom teaching: (1) educational practices often used in the classroom lack a research base to justify use to meet purported needs, or (2) educational practices are appropriate to meet purported needs but are not implemented in a manner in which they were developed. As a result, interventions used with struggling learners need to be selected primarily as a result of "students' actual performance in class" (Brown-Chidsey & Steege, 2005, p. 11). As discussed, decision making within multi-tiered response to intervention begins with universal screening and for those who exhibit struggling behaviors continues into the identification of specific needs (e.g., phonemic awareness, behavior supports) to best provide Tier 2 supplemental supports. The multi-tiered RTI assessment decisions subsequently move into the ongoing progress-monitoring stage followed by diagnostic assessments to determine eligibility for special education should the learner continue to make inadequate progress with supplemental and intensive interventions.

Assessment Implications

Both the instructional and decision-making components of multi-tiered response to intervention have direct assessment implications for struggling learners. These include:

1. Implementation of evidence-based interventions must occur along with conducting response to intervention assessment.

2. Use of research-based assessment practices is necessary to adequately determine response to instruction.

3. Interventions must be implemented in the classroom in the manner in which they were researched and validated prior to making judgments that a student is struggling in school.

4. If appropriate evidence-based instruction is not provided to a struggling learner, it must be implemented prior to using assessment data to make instructional decisions.

5. Collection of frequent and regular assessment data reflecting student progress forms the foundation for basing decisions concerning the level and intensity of instruction a learner should receive.

To meet these assessment demands within multi-tiered response to intervention, educators must select and implement a problem-solving model that best meets a variety of diverse needs exhibited by students in today's classrooms.

MULTI-TIERED RESPONSE TO INTERVENTION DECISION-MAKING MODELS

As discussed, the student's rate of progress and level of achievement to meet curricular objectives or benchmarks dictate the level of instruction most appropriate for the learner. Within multi-tiered instruction, the process for making decisions is just as critical as the process for monitoring progress and charting data. Educator teams involved with response to intervention must engage in one of three decision-making models discussed in the literature (Fuchs & Fuchs, 2006; Marston, Reschly, Lau, Muyskens, & Canter, 2007). Table 1.2 summarizes the three model types.

Table 1.2   Multi-Tiered Response to Intervention Decision-Making Models

Model	Description	Analysis
Standard Treatment	Use of the same treatment for all learners with similar needs (e.g., phonemic awareness, self-monitoring); instructional decisions are based primarily on data resulting from the standard treatment intervention.	More rigorous and accurate in identifying special needs than problem-solving model; procedure is more selective and may miss identifying some students with special needs.
Problem Solving	Process of identifying individual needs followed by development of implementation program; instructional decisions are made by problem-solving team, using additional ecological information about individual learner to clarify and pinpoint needs.	Less rigorous than Standard Treatment model yet is able to include most/all students with special needs; runs risk of misidentifying some students as having special needs when they do not.
Combined Standard Treatment/ Problem Solving	Process in which elements of both models are used to make decisions and provide appropriate level of instruction; decisions are made by problem-solving team using standard treatment data and other related information to best understand learner needs.	Draws upon strengths of both models which allows problem-solving teams to base instructional decisions on standard treatment data along with considerations of other ecological variables; more time-intensive than other models.

As shown, each of the three decision-making models contain strengths as well as some limitations (Fuchs & Fuchs, 2006). The standard treatment model is more rigorous and more accurate in identifying special needs; however, it may miss some learners in the process. The problem-solving model considers a variety of ecological factors to best understand learner needs and captures most learners with special needs; however, it may mistakenly include some learners as having special needs when they do not. The combined model allows problem-solving teams to employ the strengths of both models to develop and implement a comprehensive plan for the learner; however, it is a more time-consuming model. The problem-solving and combined models also promote the concept that "one size doesn't fit all"—a concept that the standard treatment model does not emphasize. This distinction is especially important since response to instruction results may eventually lead to a referral and possible placement of the learner into special education, such as learning disabilities (Bender & Shores, 2007; Fuchs, 2003). (Chapter 7 provides a more detailed coverage of the use of the combined model.)

The overview presentation of multi-tiered response to intervention presented in this chapter is designed to provide the reader a summary of this increasing educational practice in our schools, with specific reference to the assessment process for making instructional and/or diagnostic decisions. (The reader is referred to the following sources for additional information about tiered instruction and response to intervention: Fuchs & Fuchs, 2006; Haager, Klingner, & Vaughn, 2007, Hoover & Patton, 2008; Jimerson, Burns, & VanDerHeyden, 2007; Vaughn, 2003; Vaughn, Linan-Thompson, & Hickman, 2003; Wright, 2007). This chapter concludes with three checklists, developed from content found in the above sources, for readers to evaluate their schools' multi-tiered response to intervention process (see Forms 1.1, 1.2, and 1.3).

As reflected in Form 1.1, a variety of elements must be addressed to successfully implement the process within each tier in a multi-tiered response to intervention model in today's schools. Readers are encouraged to apply this form to their specific situations to gain a general overview of their school's multi-tiered process. Collectively, the following summarize key aspects of multi-tiered response to intervention for which assessment teams must make critical decisions:

1. Extent to which the learner is meeting curricular benchmarks/objectives (includes both rate of progress and level of meeting targeted objectives).

2. Tier (of intervention) to provide to the learner based on data demonstrating progress toward meeting benchmarks/objectives.

3. Effectiveness of evidence-based interventions on student progress (i.e., RTI).

4. Eligibility for formal special education assessment and/or placement for a disability.

Form 1.2 (RTI Baseline Assessment Guide) is a guide for documenting whether the most critical elements necessary to successfully implement RTI exist within a school. This guide assists school teams to determine the RTI components that exist in their schools along with the training that has been provided to its educators. Those components not addressed serve as a basis for structuring an RTI Action Plan (Form 1.3).

As shown, users of Form 1.2 initially document specific RTI components that are in place and the training that has been completed with school personnel. These tasks reflect the primary components within RTI that require development, implementation, and associated professional development. This is followed by the identification and documentation of specific RTI tasks to be completed. Different tasks should be documented as the overall process of implementing RTI is undertaken. Since it will take an extended period of time (e.g., three–five years) to successfully incorporate all necessary RTI aspects into the total school, the development and implementation of different RTI tasks should be documented on an action plan to guide progress toward a comprehensive schoolwide RTI structure to meet the needs of all students. Information clarified and documented on Forms 1.1, 1.2, and 1.3 provide important knowledge to assessment teams and serves as a foundation for developing and implementing an effective RTI assessment process for all learners.

The remainder of this book provides more detailed coverage of various assessment procedures and practices within multi-tiered response to intervention necessary to best meet a variety of learner needs as key decisions in the above four areas are made by assessment or child study teams.

SUMMARY

Multi-tiered response to intervention is quickly becoming the preferred instructional practice to meet the needs of learners at risk and those struggling in school. The underlying premise of this practice is that students must be provided levels of instruction that increase in duration and intensity as progress-monitoring data indicate. Fundamental to this overall practice is the need for educators to gather, record, and chart data reflecting students' progress toward meeting established district curricular benchmarks and related objectives. Three problem-solving models exist within multi-tiered RTI, with the combined standard treatment and problem-solving approaches providing the best opportunities for educators to meet needs of all learners in today's classrooms.

Applying Chapter 1 Learning Outcomes

1. Using Form 1.1, conduct an evaluation of your school's multi-tiered RTI model to determine its comprehensive structure to meet needs of all learners.

2. Discuss the strengths and concerns in using each of the three problem-solving models discussed in the chapter.

3. Identify your personal strengths and areas needing further development to best implement multi-tiered instruction in your classroom; develop and complete a professional development plan.

4. Complete an analysis of your school's overall assessment decision-making points and determine the process for making assessment decisions.

Form 1.1 Checklist for Essential Multi-Tiered Response to Intervention Elements

Instructions: Check each element for each tier prior to implementing a different level of instruction to ensure effective implementation of multi-tiered RTI.

Tier 1 Core Instructional Elements

_____ All students are instructed in the general education classroom using evidence-based curriculum and interventions.

_____ Universal screening is conducted for all students three times per year using research-based assessment procedures and practices.

_____ Rate of student progress toward achieving curricular benchmarks is considered relative to anticipated expectations in addition to universal screening results.

_____ Students who fail to make adequate rates of progress and/or fall below established cut-off scores for universal screening (e.g., those in the lowest 25th percentile) are identified for Tier 2 supplemental supports.

Tier 2 Supplemental Instructional Elements

_____ Learners are provided targeted, supplemental instructional support to complement the Tier 1 core general class curriculum.

_____ Process for monitoring the effects of supplemental instruction is identified and carried out (e.g., monthly/bi-weekly monitoring).

_____ Student response to the supplemental instruction is determined through the gathering of data within the monitoring process identified.

_____ Progress-monitoring data are charted to visually illustrate student progress over time.

_____ Student rate of progress is determined and compared to expected rate of progress based on learning needs.

_____ A second round of Tier 2 supplemental supports is completed if student initially fails to make adequate progress with initial supports provided.

_____ Progress-monitoring data are used to base decisions on student response to Tier 2 supplemental instruction.

_____ Students not making an adequate rate of progress and who do not meet curricular benchmarks or objectives after two rounds of supplemental instruction receive Tier 3 intensive interventions.

Tier 3 Intensive Intervention Elements

_____ Students receive evidence-based and appropriate intensive interventions to meet individual needs identified through Tier 2 progress monitoring and other relevant diagnostic assessment.

_____ Student progress is monitored and charted on a highly frequent basis (e.g., daily, three times per week).

___ Students considered for special education are provided all due process procedures and safeguards as mandated by IDEA (2004).

___ Student IEPs are generated for those determined to have a disability that includes appropriate evidence-based interventions, progress-monitoring procedures, and related diagnostic measures to clarify and pinpoint individual needs.

___ Progress-monitoring data are used to base decisions on student response to Tier 3 intensive interventions.

___ Students are only provided Tier 3 interventions for as long as necessary, and return to Tier 2 or 1 instructional levels as soon as rate of progress and achievement of benchmarks or objectives are satisfactory.

Summary of Multi-Tiered Instruction:

Form 1.2 Checklist for RTI Baseline Assessment

RTI Leader: _____ Date: _____

School/District: _____

Instructions: Check each component/training aspect currently in place pertaining to RTI in your school (*check all that apply*):

I. RTI Components

____ Universal screening of all students is in place.

____ Tier 1 core research-based instruction is identified in all grades (*check areas*):

    ____ Reading

    ____ Mathematics

    ____ Writing

    ____ Science

    ____ Social Studies

____ Tier 2 supplemental level of instruction is clarified.

____ Tier 3 intensive level of intervention is clarified.

____ Implementation of evidence-based interventions occurs in all classrooms.

____ Process for determining fidelity of implementation of interventions/curricula is identified.

____ Process for determining fidelity of implementation of assessment is identified.

____ Classroom progress-monitoring procedures are in place.

____ RTI problem-solving decision-making team has been established.

____ Process for identifying students requiring Tier 2 or 3 intervention is established.

____ Rate of progress is defined for each subject/grade.

____ Data-based decision-making process is established.

____ Process for considering cultural and linguistic needs of diverse learners is established.

____ Process for referring and determining eligibility for special education is in place.

____ Schoolwide behavior-supports plan exists.

____ Gap analysis procedures are clarified

____ Other:

II. RTI Training

All educators have received RTI training in the following (*check all that apply*):

____ Universal screening

____ Progress-monitoring procedures and charting of results (e.g., CBM)

____ Each tier/level of instruction (Tier 1, 2, and 3)

____ Knowledge/skills to implement education with fidelity

____ Process for determining fidelity of implementation of interventions/curricula

____ Process for determining fidelity of implementation of assessment

____ RTI problem-solving decision-making team procedures

____ Process for identifying students needing Tiers 2 or 3 levels of intervention

____ Classroom teacher roles/responsibilities in implementing tiered instruction

____ Data-based decision-making process and procedures

____ Process for referring and determining eligibility for special education

____ Positive behavioral supports/functional behavioral assessment

____ Gap analysis and rate of progress

____ Other:

Form 1.3   RTI Action Plan

Educator Completing Form: _____ Date: _____

School/District:_____

Instructions: Record the RTI task to be developed and implemented.

I. Clarifying the RTI Task

RTI task to be developed/implemented (briefly describe):

Location of RTI task to be completed:

Summarize expectations regarding development of this task.

Summarize existing situation regarding RTI task (e.g., aspects currently in place, preliminary planning).

Describe school/district support currently in place to complete task.

What support is needed that currently does not exist?

II. Clarifying the Process for Completing RTI Task

What changes must occur to successfully complete RTI task?

Which educators are most impacted by these changes?

What RTI materials do you currently have?

What other RTI materials do you need to complete task?

Who will you need to work with directly to complete your task?

List steps/timeline to follow to complete RTI task:

Task   Date to Be Completed By

1. _____

2. _____

3. _____

4. _____

5. _____

6. _____

Date that you have successfully completed RTI task: _____

2

Assessment Continuum in Multi-Tiered Response to Intervention

SIGNIFICANCE TO CONTEMPORARY ASSESSMENT

Although assessment of struggling learners has been an integral part of our educational system for decades, multi-tiered instruction brings a new perspective to assessment and its relationship to instruction by determining student progress in learning on an ongoing, continuous basis. Historically, assessment has been used to identify needs or problems found primarily "within" the learner where a battery of assessment measures and practices are completed, within a brief period of time, once the student demonstrates more significant needs. Through multi-tiered instructional frameworks, the emphasis of assessment is to determine the extent to which students are learning that which has been taught, rather than what is "wrong" with the learner. The significance of the assessment continuum found within multi-tiered response to intervention is that it facilitates a more direct link between instruction and progress, which facilitates more informed decisions concerning tiers or levels of instruction as well as diagnostic assessment needs, should referral for special education be warranted.

CHAPTER OVERVIEW

Chapter 2 provides discussion and details about the three primary multi-tiered RTI assessment decision points implemented along a continuum. These are referred to as *universal screening, progress monitoring,* and *diagnostic assessment.* These three practices form the assessment foundation in multi-tiered response to intervention. This chapter discusses the essential aspects necessary to successfully implement each of these three types of assessments.

Key Topics Addressed in Chapter

✦ Role of Assessment in Multi-Tiered Instruction

✦ Universal Screening

✦ Progress Monitoring

✦ Diagnostic Assessment

✦ Assessment Reliability, Validity, Fairness, and Fidelity

LEARNER OUTCOMES

Upon completion of Chapter 2, readers will

- understand the integral role assessment assumes in multi-tiered instruction
- be knowledgeable about universal screening procedures and outcomes
- acquire skills necessary to monitor student progress in the classroom
- be familiar with the interaction between implementation of evidence-based interventions and ongoing progress monitoring
- be knowledgeable of competencies needed to implement various assessments on the assessment continuum

PERSONAL PERSPECTIVE

A primary underlying component of multi-tiered response to intervention is the use of assessment data to base educational decisions to assist struggling learners. My experiences in working with educators in assessment have helped me to see some of the advances and concerns related to assessment within RTI. Perhaps the most significant value-added assessment aspect we see in today's schools is screening to identify at-risk and struggling learners early in their schooling. This process, referred to as "universal screening," provides educators with valuable information about learners who are struggling to make adequate progress toward identified benchmarks or objectives. Through this process, struggling learners receive much needed academic support early in their education—support that was previously often not provided until more significant problems

(Continued)

(Continued)

emerged. It is encouraging to see the increased efforts that have been under-taken in this important area.

Another important aspect of assessment currently being implemented in schools pertains to the regular and more frequent monitoring of student progress throughout the academic year. This "progress monitoring" is completed to more closely assess connections between that which is taught and how students are progressing in learning. Through my trainings and related work with educators, I have seen two issues that require attention to ensure that the most effective progress monitoring occurs: (1) teachers require support and training to efficiently conduct progress monitoring within the parameters of daily implementation of curriculum, and (2) in some instances, a disconnect exists between that which is taught and what is assessed. Progress monitoring is designed to assess what students have learned relative to that which is taught, and if what is assessed is not directly connected to content and skills taught, the monitoring results may be misleading. I have found that direct training in these areas helps teachers see the connections between what is taught and assessed and this leads to more meaningful monitoring of results. This includes helping educators understand the continuum of assessment discussed in this chapter, along with specific preparation to implement progress-monitoring procedures that will be discussed later in this book (e.g., curriculum-based measurement).

ROLE OF ASSESSMENT IN MULTI-TIERED RESPONSE TO INTERVENTION

As previously emphasized in the overview of multi-tiered instruction presented in Chapter 1, accurate and ongoing assessment provides the foundation for effective decision making for struggling learners. To best internalize the critical role assessment assumes in tiered instruction, it is important to discuss the change in the perspective of assessment and struggling learners.

Historical Perspective of Assessment

Throughout the past several decades, the primary role of assessment in the education of struggling learners has been one of attempting to identify potential "deficits" within the learner, while simultaneously assuming that lack of progress toward academic or social-emotional benchmarks or objectives was predominately due to something going on "within" the learner. Some key components of this approach to assessment include: (1) waiting for the learner to demonstrate sufficient deficiencies prior to conducting a more complete assessment; (2) conducting assessment primarily in a decontextualized setting (i.e., use of devices and practices that had little or no direct connection to actual classroom instruction); (3) the presumption that struggling learners were always provided appropriate instruction using the most relevant strategies and differentiation methods; and (4) explaining the lack of progress by focusing on intrinsic student characteristics rather than on the observable instructional environment, including curriculum implemented teaching strategies, opportunities to learn, and other ecological factors which will be discussed in Chapter 3.

Over time, the results of this "deficit assessment model" were: (1) a significant increase in the number of students who went two or three years struggling in learning before concentrated attention was paid to their needs; (2) increases in the number of students placed in special education since this model is predicated on the refer, test, and place concept; and (3) significant numbers of students falling farther behind in academics, particularly in the area of reading, resulting from the lack of timely supplemental support and/or consideration of the significance of the lack of high quality instruction. Due to these and other related issues, the need to refocus assessment of student progress gradually began to change from one of "deficit" to "quality of instruction," leading to the current emphasis in today's schools.

Contemporary Perspective of Assessment

In today's instructional environments, a significant amount of emphasis is placed on high-quality teaching, research-based curriculum, evidence-based interventions, gathering and charting performance data, and student progress toward achieving that which is directly taught in the classroom. These above factors provide the core of multi-tiered RTI as summarized in Chapter 1. However, a significant departure from the previous "deficit assessment model" is the practice of screening early, pinpointing needs early, providing timely supplemental support based on these early assessments, and continuously monitoring progress. Therefore, the contemporary view toward assessment is one that includes: (1) regular schoolwide or *universal screening*; (2) closely monitoring students who demonstrate initial needs from the universal screening; (3) frequent assessments or *progress monitoring* provided for learners to more closely track their progress; and (4) providing a more comprehensive or *diagnostic assessment* only after the variables of effective curriculum, effective instruction, and adequate learning opportunities to make progress have not resulted in a sufficient rate of progress and/or a minimum proficiency level in achieving desired benchmarks or objectives.

In short, a primary difference between the historical and contemporary approaches to assessment in today's schools is found in its emphasis on proper instruction first, rather than initially believing that there is something wrong within the student when insufficient academic or social-emotional progress is observed. This, along with more timely and continuous assessment to identify needs and progress, reflects major differences between previous and current assessment in today's schools. The contemporary model of assessment within multi-tiered response to intervention can be viewed as a process that occurs along a continuum, progressing from initial screening of all students to the monitoring of progress for a select group of struggling learners to individual diagnostic assessment for those who exhibit more significant needs. This assessment continuum is illustrated below.

Universal Screening	Progress Monitoring	Diagnostic Assessment
Tier 1	Tiers 1/2/3	Tiers 2/3

Each of these three primary types of multi-tiered assessments reflect: (1) scope of assessment, (2) timing of assessment, (3) purpose of the assessment, (4) intended uses of the assessment scores or results, and (5) critical points for decisions concerning the level and intensity of instruction the learner requires. Discussed below is a more detailed account of each of these three types of assessment where the essential aspects are highlighted. Information presented in each of the following descriptions were derived from content found in several sources (Bender & Shores, 2007; Brown-Chidsey & Steege 2005; Johnson, Mellard, Fuchs, & McKnight, 2006; Mellard & Johnson, 2008). However, prior to discussing these assessments, the topics of assessment reliability, validity, fairness, and fidelity will be summarized. Knowledge about each of these is essential to effective assessment since these form the foundation for acquiring accurate scores or results. A general understanding of these concepts empowers educators to conduct assessment with integrity as well as interpret scores within relevant education contexts.

Assessment Reliability

Reliability in assessment refers to the extent to which assessment results (i.e., scores) are consistent over time (McMillan, 2001). This includes the consistency with which "an instrument measures an ability" (Wallace & Hammill, p. 43, 2002). Therefore, assessment reliability includes determination of the assessment device's and/or processes' ability to yield consistent results across time and under various situations. Reliability is presented as a "reliability coefficient" in which a coefficient of .80 or greater is considered necessary to ensure adequate reliability (Wallace & Hammill). It is important to keep in mind that reliability refers to consistency in scores obtained over time and it is critical for assessment teams to determine reliability in order to make valid and informed assessment decisions. That is, universal screening, progress monitoring, and diagnostic assessment (both devices and processes) must each yield reliable (i.e., consistent) scores to be of assessment significance to accurately determine student responses to instruction.

Assessment Validity

Validity in assessment is crucial to making informed and accurate decisions about a student's responses to instruction and to make recommendations for the most appropriate level or tier of intervention. While complex in nature, an initial concern is that an assessment device and/or assessment practice is considered valid if it does what it purports to do (Wallace & Hammill, 2002). An assessment device must be valid for what it says it measures (e.g., oral reading fluency, science concepts). However, this type of validity refers only to the device or practice; a subsequent issue with validity refers to the uses of the obtained scores or results. An instrument may be valid for measuring a defined ability (e.g., math computation); yet, the overall assessment validity may be flawed if the obtained scores are used for purposes other than those recommended by developers of the instrument or practice.

For example, if an assessment instrument is designed primarily to assess a learner's abilities with phonics and the results are also used to determine vocabulary levels, then the assessment *scores* are used to not only determine student progress with phonics but also to assess vocabulary. If the assessment device in our example was not validated to assess vocabulary development, the use of those scores for this purpose is not valid. The instrument in our example is validated to assess and determine levels of phonics abilities and should be used primarily for this purpose. McMillan (2001) refers to this type of situation as "validity of the inference from test scores" (p. 17).

Therefore, assessment teams must determine validity from at least two different perspectives: (1) that the instrument or practice used in the learning environment is valid for how it is actually used in multi-tiered response to intervention assessment, and (2) that the uses of and inferences from the obtained assessment scores are applied in a manner consistent with the purposes for which the assessment device/practice was validated. As a result, validity of the assessment instrument/practice as well as validity of the uses of the obtained assessment scores must be present to make accurate multi-tiered RTI decisions for students struggling with learning. Similar to reliability, universal screening, progress monitoring, and diagnostic assessment (both devices/practices and inferences from obtained scores) must be valid for their intended purposes and uses to be of assessment significance to accurately determine student responses to instruction.

Assessment Fairness

Fundamental to effective assessment within multi-tiered response to intervention is implementation of a fair assessment process. This includes use of fair and unbiased assessment devices and practices, consideration of various ecological factors (e.g., student, classroom, home/community) as well as ecological validity (See Chapter 3).

Assessment Fidelity

Fidelity refers to the implementation of instruction, assessment or other defined practice in the manner consistent with the way each practice was designed and recommended to be implemented (e.g., following the test's standard assessment procedures when administering that test, completing all recommended steps in the proper order) (Hoover, 2009; Mellard & Johnson, 2008). In regards to assessment, fidelity indicates: (1) that the assessment device and/or practice is implemented according to the validated procedures discussed in the manual or related write-up, (2) that the obtained assessment scores are used for purposes consistent with the way they are recommended to be used as determined through the validity studies, and (3) ecological factors are considered to ensure the most appropriate and informed decision making occurs.

In essence, *fidelity of assessment* in multi-tiered response to intervention refers to the proper implementation of the assessment practices, procedures, and devices along with accurately drawing proper inferences from obtained assessment scores. As previously described for both reliability and validity, universal screening, progress monitoring, and diagnostic assessment must each be implemented with fidelity to be of assessment significance to accurately determine student responses to instruction. Due to the significance of assessment fidelity in multi-tiered RTI, this topic is further discussed in Chapter 4. It is introduced here to encourage readers to appreciate the importance of this concept early in our discussions.

UNIVERSAL SCREENING

Definition: Universal screening is a form of assessment that is easy to administer, low cost, and can be periodically repeated providing valid data on student progress on selected academic and/or social-emotional benchmarks. It is a "process that uses short, quick, and easy-to-administer probes that are aligned to the curriculum and measure specific skills a student has achieved" (McCook, 2006, p. 13).

Purpose: The primary purpose of universal screening in multi-tiered instruction is to initially identify learners at risk or those who may be showing early signs of struggling with learning who require further attention and investigation into the suspected need. In addition to identifying struggling learners, the National Association of State Directors of Special Education (NASDSE) (2005) wrote that universal screening assists to identify those teachers who may require support in meeting needs in their classrooms.

Significance in Multi-Tiered Response to Intervention: Universal screening provides the initial evidence to educators that a learner may be struggling as well as the initial decision-making point concerning the most appropriate level or tier of instruction.

Implementation Process: Universal screening is implemented in a variety of ways ranging from one administration annually at the beginning of each academic year to three times per year (i.e., beginning, middle, end). Concerns with the once-per-year administration are that some learners whose scores indicate below performance may require additional time (e.g., four–six weeks) to demonstrate satisfactory progress. In this instance, providing the learner Tier 2 supplemental support would not be necessary, yet this would occur if only one administration is conducted. To deal with this potential situation, Compton, Fuchs, Fuchs, and Bryant (2006) suggest that learners identified as at risk through a once per year universal screening model should be monitored on a weekly basis for a few weeks (e.g., four–six weeks) to confirm the at risk status initially indicated by the universal screening. This process serves to continue monitoring learner progress while also ensuring that Tier 2 supplemental support is necessary. Another alternative to the one-time universal screening that is supported by many educators is the repeated screening model where the universal screening occurs three times per year.

Primary Uses of Results: Universal screening results provide data for identifying learners at risk and those who require additional monitoring. This may include decisions to continue with Tier 1 instruction or begin to provide supplemental Tier 2 support. Initial universal screening also provides the baseline data for future comparison of growth.

Decision-Making Specifics: Universal screening data lead to decisions in several areas: (1) comparison to a pre-established "cut score" below which learners are considered at risk—cut scores generally range from the lowest 10 percent to the lowest 25th percentile and are established by individual states or school systems; (2) determination of the student's rate of progress using baseline universal screening for comparison; and (3) clarification of need to implement Tier 2 supplemental support.

Significance for Struggling Learners: Universal screening provides learners who are struggling in school the opportunity to be identified early in their struggles. It alerts educators early in the school year of those who potentially may be at risk for problems with learning. Most important, universal screening provides struggling learners necessary support, if needed, prior to falling significantly farther behind.

PROGRESS MONITORING

Definition: Progress monitoring is a research-based method that facilitates the assessment of learner academic and/or social-emotional progress on a regular and consistent basis.

Purpose: The primary purposes of progress monitoring are to determine the extent to which students are learning that which is being taught and effectiveness of instruction. More specifically, progress monitoring determines both level of achievement (e.g., number of words read correctly) as well as rate of improvement or progress (e.g., student shows consistent increase in number of words read correctly) for the purpose of implementing more effective education to students. Progress monitoring may be used to assess progress of both individual students as well as whole classrooms of learners.

Significance in Multi-Tiered Response to Intervention: Progress-monitoring data provides multi-tiered instructional teams with immediate, easy to gather classroom-based assessment results that directly reflect actual instruction, in order to determine the extent that classroom instruction is effective in helping students progress in learning. These results, in turn, serve as one important source used to make informed, data-based decisions concerning the most appropriate level, duration, and intensity of instruction required to meet learner needs in Tiers 1, 2, or 3. Curriculum-based measurement (CBM) is one progress-monitoring assessment practice that many school systems have implemented. CBM is discussed in detail as one effective progress-monitoring method in Chapter 5.

Implementation Process: Progress monitoring is a standardized approach where repeated assessments using parallel or similar devices or practices (assessing the same target skill) are completed over a defined period of time. While universal screening is generally completed three times per year, progress monitoring is implemented much more frequently, such as monthly, bimonthly, weekly, or even daily depending on the needs of the learners. To implement progress monitoring the steps below are followed:

- Identify skill to be monitored (e.g., oral reading fluency, math computation skills).
- Select/develop valid assessment measures to quickly assess skills (e.g., one–two minutes) that directly reflect the instruction of the target skills (e.g., oral reading passage at second grade level).
- Determine monitoring schedule (e.g., monthly, weekly).
- Conduct assessment adhering to the established schedule.
- Graph or chart the results of each assessment.
- Evaluate level of performance and rate of progress (e.g., progress toward developing math computation abilities).
- Adjust instruction based on progress-monitoring data.
- Continue with ongoing progress monitoring, chart results, and adjust instruction as needed.

Primary Uses of Results: Progress-monitoring results are indicators of effectiveness of instruction. Should the learner demonstrate inadequate progress, then a change in the instruction is indicated (Mellard & Johnson, 2008). Therefore, a primary use of progress-monitoring data is to adjust instruction as indicated by student progress toward achievement of targeted skills. This relates directly to quality, fidelity, and effectiveness of instruction in Tiers 1, 2, or 3.

Decision-Making Specifics: Progress-monitoring data assist to answer several key instructional questions: (1) How effective is the instruction? (2) How is the student progressing relative to others in the classroom or grade? (3) Should a change in instruction be implemented? and (4) Does the student require more intensive interventions? By conducting regular and frequent assessments of student progress, responses to these and related questions may more easily be obtained in a timely and objective manner.

Significance for Struggling Learners: Ongoing progress monitoring is highly significant to the education of struggling learners due to the immediate and frequent gathering of data reflecting student progress. Progress monitoring represents a significant change in the assessment of struggling learners in that their needs are more quickly identified and monitored over time, rather than only after continued and persistent failures with little adjustment to instruction. Progress-monitoring procedures are also significant to struggling learners in that greater clarity concerning the existence of a suspected disability is seen, reducing inappropriate referrals and/or placements for special education.

DIAGNOSTIC ASSESSMENT

Definition: Diagnostic assessment is an individualized and targeted form of assessment specific to identifying individual learner needs and/or disabilities (Pierangelo & Giuliani, 2006).

Purpose: The primary purpose of diagnostic assessment is to "diagnose" individual learning needs, strengths, and recommendations for effective instruction. In addition, diagnostic assessment results assist multi-tiered problem-solving teams to develop relevant and meaningful individual educational plans consistent with specialized instruction to meet more significant needs.

Significance in Multi-Tiered Response to Intervention: Diagnostic assessment becomes more essential as learners demonstrate insufficient progress as determined through universal screening and progress monitoring. For some learners, education through multi-tiered instruction may lead to a special education referral and associated comprehensive diagnostic assessment, due to a persistent lack of progress and continued demonstration of not adequately responding to instruction.

Implementation Process: The diagnostic assessment process actually begins during universal screening and continues through progress monitoring, resulting in the need for more specific assessment of individual needs (i.e., diagnostic). Once determined necessary by the multi-tiered response to intervention team, diagnostic assessment includes selecting and administering a variety of assessment devices and/or practices necessary to more fully understand the student's needs. This may include administration of individual diagnostic reading (e.g., Woodcock Reading Mastery Test) or math (KeyMath) assessments, continued uses of curriculum-based measurements, or task analysis as well as observations or interviews to clarify individual learning needs.

Primary Uses of Results: Unlike universal screening and progress monitoring which primarily assess effects of instruction, diagnostic assessment also looks at abilities intrinsic to the learner with results being used primarily for determining: (1) eligibility for specific services (e.g., special education), (2) pinpointing specific academic and social-emotional needs, and (3) the development of individual educational plans.

Decision-Making Specifics: Diagnostic assessment in multi-tiered instruction provides for more individual decisions about learners, including particular educational programs that may be of benefit to the student (e.g., Wilson Reading System), progress that the student makes through Tier 3 intensive interventions, or the point at which less intensive interventions are warranted.

Significance for Struggling Learners: Diagnostic assessment assumes a much more meaningful role in multi-tiered response to intervention for struggling learners since it will occur within the context of both universal screening and progress monitoring where high quality instruction is initially corroborated. Should diagnostic assessment be determined necessary, if implemented properly, learners are assured that evidence-based instruction has occurred, increasing the possibility that continued educational needs and lack of progress may be attributed to intrinsic qualities and not ineffective teaching or improper uses of curriculum. This is a significant departure from previous practices where many struggling learners continued to fail prior to being administered a battery of diagnostic assessments for the primary purpose of finding what may be "wrong" with the student, with less consideration of the quality, fidelity, or integrity of the classroom instruction.

COMPETENCIES FOR IMPLEMENTING THE CONTINUUM OF ASSESSMENT

It should be obvious that the three main assessments associated with the continuum within multi-tiered RTI are very different from that which we have been implementing with struggling learners over the past several decades. As a result, educators must reevaluate their skills and abilities pertaining to assessment to best meet current and future demands. This includes development of a working knowledge of all aspects associated with the continuum of assessment, including several competencies as discussed below.

Competency 1: Purpose for the Assessment. Knowledge of the characteristics and qualities of universal screening, progress monitoring, and diagnostic assessment provides a solid foundation for ensuring successful implementation and meaningful participation. Familiarizing oneself with *why* these three types of assessments exist within the broader parameters of effective education is critical to proper implementation. Essentially, this refers to a continuum that begins with screening, proceeds to ongoing monitoring, and may eventually result in a more comprehensive diagnostic assessment. However, we must keep in mind that this process or continuum will be followed for most students in today's classrooms, departing from the previous practice of moving directly into diagnostic assessment.

Competency 2: Connection Between Instruction and Assessment. Through multi-tiered RTI, initial decisions pertaining to struggling learners are grounded in the evidence that demonstrates that students were taught by properly trained teachers using research-based curricula and implemented the way the instruction was designed to be implemented. Therefore, curriculum implementation and assessment are directly connected, where assessment is designed to initially determine that the struggling student was properly taught. Should evidence exist that this was not the case then proper implementation of instruction must be completed and effects assessed prior to consideration of problems intrinsic to the student. In addition, this competency assists us to best understand that assessment within multi-tiered instruction is designed to directly assess student knowledge of that which is taught in the classroom, rather than that which might be "wrong" within the learner.

Competency 3: Procedures for Implementation. Both general and special educators will increasingly need to implement multi-tiered assessment within their classrooms. Therefore, knowledge about the manner in which universal screening, progress monitoring, and diagnostic assessments are properly conducted is essential in today's educational system. Procedures for each type of multi-tiered assessment are generally simple to implement and educators will benefit by preparing themselves to incorporate necessary assessments within their overall classroom structure to screen for at-risk learners, monitor progress, and/or diagnose significant needs.

Competency 4: Charting Results. Once assessment data are gathered, they must be charted to illustrate student progress and level of achievement. This competency reflects knowledge and skills related to the most effective way to chart or graph assessment data for both small and large groups of students. In some instances use of commercial screening and monitoring devices and associated scoring and illustration of results occurs. Whether commercial or educator developed, proper charting of multi-tiered RTI assessment results must exist. Educators who develop this competency will benefit significantly as the charting of results is completed in an efficient and time-saving manner.

Competency 5: Interpreting Results. Another assessment competency needed to effectively implement multi-tiered response to intervention is that of appropriately interpreting screening, monitoring, or diagnostic assessment results. Once assessment has been implemented and data properly charted, educators are challenged to accurately interpret the meaning and relevance of those results. Educators must possess a working knowledge of what screening, monitoring, and diagnostic results mean to assume a meaningful role in the application of assessment data to best meet learner needs through the most relevant level or tier of intervention.

Competency 6: Validity of Uses of Scores. Among all the various aspects associated with effective assessment, the use of the assessment scores is the most critical to struggling learners. All aspects of assessment may be completed with the utmost integrity; however, if the uses of the assessment scores are not valid then multi-tiered RTI cannot be implemented effectively. Professional development in this important competency assists educators to use screening, progress monitoring, and diagnostic scores only for the purposes for which they have been designed to be used. Invalid use of assessment scores leads to erroneous assessment decisions which in turn leads to inappropriate multi-tiered instruction for struggling learners.

Competency 7: Decision-Making Process. General and special class educators are often responsible for implementing multi-tiered assessments and making necessary instructional adjustments; decisions concerning the meaning and uses of assessment scores are also completed by a school or district multi-tiered assessment problem-solving team. All educators should be familiar with their school's problem-solving team and the responsibilities of that team. In addition, the process for making decisions using screening, progress monitoring, and diagnostic data is essential to effective classroom instruction. Whether directly or indirectly involved in the team decision-making process, general and special educators who have an understanding of how assessment scores will be used are best able to contribute to the overall assessment process.

Training in these competencies empowers educators working at any level or tier of intervention to become and remain an integral part of the overall assessment continuum. Form 2.1, developed from information found in the sources cited in this chapter, provides a checklist to evaluate current proficiency levels with these competencies. Additionally, Chapter 7 provides a detailed discussion of the problem-solving process in multi-tiered response to intervention to further clarify this process, as used in many school systems.

SUMMARY

Assessment results of one type or another form the foundation for making informed instructional and/or diagnostic decisions. The three primary forms of assessment include universal screening, ongoing progress monitoring, and diagnostic. These form a "continuum of assessment" where assessment becomes more frequent and more targeted as the learner fails to demonstrate sufficient levels of proficiency or adequate rate of progress toward achieving benchmarks or objectives. Seven competencies were identified as important knowledge and skill areas for educators to possess to effectively and efficiently implement the continuum of assessment within multi-tiered response to intervention.

Applying Chapter 2 Learning Outcomes

1. Compare and contrast the intended purpose for using each type of assessment: universal screening, progress monitoring, and diagnostic.

2. Lead a discussion with your assessment team on the specific decision-making outcomes that are typically generated from each type of assessment.

3. Evaluate your own problem-solving team's level of competence to complete various assessments within your multi-tiered RTI model.

4. Discuss the importance of the validity in the uses of assessment scores/results to make informed decisions concerning tier or level of intervention required to meet a struggling learner's needs.

Form 2.1 Checklist for Multi-Tiered Assessment Competencies

Instructions: Indicate your current level of proficiency for each of the following assessment competencies.

1 = Limited Proficiency

2 = Some Proficiency (e.g., possess general knowledge/abilities)

3 = Adequate Proficiency (e.g., possess some in-depth knowledge/abilities)

4 = Extensive Proficiency (e.g., possess a significant amount of knowledge/abilities)

COMPETENCY	LEVEL OF PROFICIENCY			
Universal Screening				
Understand purpose	1	2	3	4
See connection to classroom instruction	1	2	3	4
Implement proper procedures	1	2	3	4
Understand fidelity in implementation	1	2	3	4
Accurately chart results	1	2	3	4
Properly interpret results	1	2	3	4
Apply scores in valid ways	1	2	3	4
Understand types of decisions made from results	1	2	3	4
Progress Monitoring				
Understand purpose	1	2	3	4
See connection to classroom instruction	1	2	3	4
Implement proper procedures	1	2	3	4
Understand fidelity in implementation	1	2	3	4
Accurately chart results	1	2	3	4
Properly interpret results	1	2	3	4
Apply scores in valid ways	1	2	3	4
Understand types of decisions made from results	1	2	3	4
Diagnostic				
Understand purpose	1	2	3	4
See connection to classroom instruction	1	2	3	4
Implement proper procedures	1	2	3	4
Understand fidelity in implementation	1	2	3	4
Accurately chart results	1	2	3	4
Properly interpret results	1	2	3	4
Apply scores in valid ways	1	2	3	4
Understand types of decisions made from results	1	2	3	4

3

Ecological Framework Within Multi-Tiered Response to Intervention

SIGNIFICANCE TO CONTEMPORARY ASSESSMENT

Ecological variables influence many aspects of teaching and learning and these must be considered to implement a valid and reliable assessment for struggling learners in multi-tiered response to intervention. Our own perspectives on curriculum and its implementation frame our daily instructional decision making. How we view the role of the learner, the teacher, the school, and society in the overall educational process shapes how we interact with and educate our students. As a result, much of what occurs in the classroom begins from outside the school such as the family, home, and broader community. An ecological perspective in teaching and learning blends a variety of environmental factors to best understand the whole situation to make more informed, comprehensive decisions. As a result, the dynamics of the interrelationship between environmental and classroom curricular elements contributes significantly to understanding the extent to which a learner responds to interventions within a multi-tiered instructional framework. Considering the influences of various ecological factors can add value to effective assessment decision making, relative to the most appropriate level and intensity of instruction for learners struggling in school.

CHAPTER OVERVIEW

Chapter 3 includes discussion of an ecological framework for understanding and making effective assessment decisions for struggling learners. Consideration of essential ecological variables to best understand assessment results for all learners is presented along with ecological assessment validity. The ways in which an ecological perspective may contribute to RTI assessment is also discussed.

Key Topics Addressed in Chapter

✦ Ecological Framework in Education

✦ Ecological Variables in Assessment

✦ Ecological Validity

✦ Assessment Bias

✦ Implementation of Multi-Tiered Response to Intervention Within an Ecological Framework

---

LEARNER OUTCOMES

Upon completion of Chapter 3, readers will

- be knowledgeable of an ecological framework within response to intervention
- understand various ecological factors necessary for comprehensive RTI assessment
- understand ecological validity and its role in assessment
- acquire skills necessary to apply ecological variables in RTI assessment

---

PERSONAL PERSPECTIVE

Throughout my thirty-five years working and teaching in education, I have found that the interpretation of assessment results continues to challenge even the most seasoned educators. As we are all aware, assessment is an integral aspect of education—a condition that is strengthened and perpetuated within multi-tiered response to intervention. One reality that most educators will not dispute is the fact that influences beyond the control of schools contribute significantly to a learner's development and educational progress. My K–12 teaching and

(Continued)

(Continued)

supervisory experiences have afforded me the opportunity to work in both urban and rural school systems in several states with different demographics and ethnic populations. These experiences taught me the significance of various ecological factors that contribute to learner development. Ecological variables such as community experiences, early childhood development, family preferences toward education, current fads/behaviors, and the interconnectedness of school, home, and community in providing effective education are a few of the areas that I have found significant to understanding the comprehensive needs of struggling learners. By understanding and valuing different qualities students bring to the classroom, I was able to make education more relevant for my students as well as more effectively interpret their assessment results.

Assessment within multi-tiered RTI also requires ecological considerations to make the most informed decisions possible concerning academic and social-emotional progress. Through my RTI research and training efforts, I have found that some problem-solving teams and schools are struggling with the role of qualitative factors in the overall assessment process. Although the current assessment emphasis is on quantified data (e.g., reading fluency rate, number of math problems correctly completed), qualitative factors that may be associated with these data scores may be important to identify and consider to best understand the needs of struggling learners. I have found that it is through consideration of various ecological factors, such as those discussed in this chapter, that educators are able to most accurately interpret assessment data results. My suggestion to educators as they interpret the meaning of assessment results is to consider some of the ecological factors in the student's life. By doing so I have found that problem-solving teams acquire a more comprehensive understanding of not only "what" that student has learned but also "how" and "under what conditions" this learning, or lack thereof, occurs.

INTRODUCTION

One of the underlying concerns with multi-tiered response to intervention assessment is the "one size doesn't fit all" concept. In essence, this refers to the notion that the exact same assessment device or process may not be appropriate for all learners. As a result, educators must make certain that if they use the same assessment devices and procedures to screen, monitor progress, as well as diagnose for possible disability, they must ensure that these are the best methods of choice to avoid perpetuation of misidentification of needs or misinterpretation of assessment results.

One educational framework that facilitates the consideration of a variety of variables when interpreting assessment results is referred to as the ecological model (Bronfenbrenner, 1995, 1979). Through this model, several interrelated factors are addressed by assessment teams, which contribute to and/or influence student progress in learning. An ecological perspective is essential to meeting diverse needs and providing comprehensive assessment for all learners within multi-tiered response to intervention.

ECOLOGICAL FRAMEWORK AND THE ASSESSMENT PROCESS

In an ecological assessment framework, factors reflective of the student's total environment are considered relative to teaching and learning needs. According to Bronfenbrenner (1995), environmental influences may significantly affect meeting the educational needs of students. The environmental factors are classified within four general types of systems as discussed below (Bronfenbrenner, 2005, 1995, 1979). Table 3.1 summarizes these systems which move from micro to macro influences upon the child and associated education.

Table 3.1   Ecological Systems and Relevance to Assessment

System	Description	Significant Influence	Relevance to Assessment
Micro	Patterns of activities, roles and relationships learner experiences in any individual setting.	The relevance to the learner of that which is experienced in any individual setting such as home, playground, store, or similar real-life settings assists in the foundation for development and growth. The *microsystem* includes both the physical setting characteristics as well as how these characteristics are perceived by the student, and more important the "meaning" that the activities, roles, and relationships hold for the individual.	An understanding of the meanings learners attach to their activities, roles, or relationships assists in interpreting assessment results as these are put into a relevant context for the student. That is, the manner in which the learner perceives the environmental experiences is significantly more important than the physical characteristics and these perceptions affect assessment results.
Meso	The interrelationship among individual settings (i.e., micro) constitute the *mesosystem* such as the learner's relationships with home, community, and school.	As learners move across settings, their experiences become integrated which further shape the "meanings" initially developed in the *microsystem*. Knowledge and attitudes become more refined as activities, roles, and relationships become more integrated through experiences across settings.	Building on the *micro*, understanding that as learner experiences expand so will the attitudes and knowledge associated with those experiences. Assessment teams must interpret assessment scores within parameters that recognize interrelated contexts rather than one individual setting or context (e.g., relationships between home and classroom values/norms).

(Continued)

Table 3.1 (Continued)

System	Description	Significant Influence	Relevance to Assessment
Exo	*Exosystem* refers to those settings that do not directly involve the learner as an active participant (e.g., a sibling's school, a parent's workplace).	While the learners are not directly influenced by *exosystem* settings, they may be indirectly affected through interactions with a person who is directly involved in that setting (e.g., problems that a parent experiences in the workplace may indirectly affect the student due to parental behaviors at home resulting from the problems on the job). In this example, the learner is not directly influenced by that which occurs at a parent's workplace yet may be indirectly affected (e.g., parent is preoccupied with work and spends less time with student).	The *exosystem* element emphasizes the importance of understanding *mesosytems* of those who the learner interacts with, as well as the *mesosystems* of the student. Influences upon the learner from *exosystems* may be very powerful in shaping the individual, which in turn provides insight into putting assessment results into the proper context to make the most relevant interpretation and uses of assessment results.
Macro	A *macrosystem* includes the three systems of micro, meso, and exo within a specific culture or subculture.	A *macrosystem* collectively includes characteristic beliefs, lifestyles, life path options, social interaction patterns, or opportunities in life. Depending upon the specific *macrosystem*, these life issues may be more or less limited for individuals. Also, similar *macrosystems* across cultures may have similar limits or opportunities (e.g., affluent families in many different cultures are afforded similar opportunities while less affluent families often experience similar limits in regards to schooling, employment, or mobility).	Awareness of the *macrosystem* to which a learner has been most exposed provides valuable insight into the assessment results, especially as these relate to opportunities to learn and experiential background relative to the assessed knowledge, skills or abilities. Knowledge of cross-cultural *macrosystems* is especially important to discern learning differences from disabilities in culturally and linguistically diverse learners who struggle in school.

Within the ecological model as described by Bronfenbrenner (1995), each of these systems provide layers or levels of influence on a child's development, progressing from the child's most immediate environment to the broader cultural norms and values. This process eventually leads to broader transitions within the environments. For comprehensive coverage of ecological perspectives in development and education, the reader is referred to Bronfenbrenner (2005, 1995, 1979) and Moen, Elder and Luscher (1995). In considering these ecological levels of influence, Hoover, Klingner et al. (2008) described three primary factors that reflect a broad environmental context that captures essential aspects of the four systems described in Table 3.1, relative to making important assessment decisions.

Student Factors

These refer to elements such as experiential background and prior educational experiences. Student factors also include consideration of student's preferred styles of learning (e.g., cooperative versus independent, study of the whole versus discrete parts) as well as emphasis on use of higher order thinking skills in learning (e.g., synthesis, evaluation, comprehension). Although a variety of student factors exist and need to be considered when identifying learning needs, educators must internalize the concept that students develop through the influences of interrelated ecological structures within which they exist (Reschly, Coolong-Chaffin, Christenson, & Gutkin, 2007). Influences from different aspects of the students' lives facilitate development and provide valuable explanations for learning strengths and needs.

Classroom Factors

A variety of classroom factors must be considered to best understand student needs within multi-tiered RTI. Ysseldyke and Christenson (2002) identified several classroom instructional factors that contribute to an ecological perspective to education. These include instructional expectations, feedback, academic learning time, adaptations, and strategies for motivation. Each of these is essential to consider to best understand and interpret multi-tiered RTI assessment results.

Home/Community Factors

A major premise of ecological theory is that a student exists and develops within a broader context that includes home and community as well as the classroom (Bronfenbrenner, 1995). Factors such as cultural values and norms, views toward education, preferences toward learning, or adjustment to new environments (Hoover, Klingner et al., 2008) are examples of home/community aspects that must be considered by multi-tiered RTI assessment teams to best understand student strengths, needs, and preferences toward styles of teaching and learning.

Multi-tiered response to intervention assessment teams who view these three ecological variables as integrated within a student's overall teaching and learning development are best informed of learner needs. This is particularly significant when interpreting data reflecting response to instruction based on universal screening, progress monitoring, and/or diagnostic assessment.

ECOLOGICAL DECISION MAKING IN MULTI-TIERED RESPONSE TO INTERVENTION

Table 3.2 provides a summary of selected factors to consider to best implement an ecologically based assessment process within multi-tiered response to intervention.

Table 3.2 Critical Factors in Ecological RTI Decision Making

Factor	RTI Decision-Making Considerations
Cultural Values and Norms	Broad cultural values and norms that students bring to the learning situation significantly shape student's development and learning.
Appropriate Evidence-Based Assessment	The selection and use of evidence-based assessment devices and practices must reflect cultural values and norms, experiential background, and opportunities to learn the knowledge and skills.
Experiential Background	Educators must understand a learner's prior experiences and obtained prerequisite skills to best determine appropriateness of rate of progress and level of achievement.
Higher Order Thinking	Ecological assessment must include documentation of evidence that instruction is cognitively challenging to the learners.
Sufficient Opportunities to Learn	Multi-tiered response to intervention teams must ensure that students are provided sufficient opportunity to master assessed knowledge and skills prior to determining lack of adequate progress toward benchmarks or objectives.
Instructional Elements	Ecological assessment considers a variety of instructional conditions important to effective development including sufficient academic learning time, instructional feedback on progress, appropriate differentiations, and use of motivational strategies.
Preferences Toward Learning	Students vary in the ways they prefer to learn and be taught. Some students prefer cooperative learning over competitive forms of instruction, group work over independent study, or initially the study of the "whole" over individual and discrete aspects of a task.

Quantified data often need to be *qualified* to make the most informed decisions for struggling learners; adherence to an ecological framework facilitates this process. Along with classroom-based data, an ecological perspective and framework in assessment assists teams to identify the most appropriate

1. tier of instruction.

2. evidence-based academic and behavioral interventions.

3. assessment devices and practices to determine response to instruction.

4. time for a referral to special education based on problems intrinsic to the learner.

5. diagnosis, should a disability be evident (Hoover, 2009).

ECOLOGICAL ASSESSMENT IN MULTI-TIERED RESPONSE TO INTERVENTION

As discussed, levels of intervention are based on assessment data obtained through ongoing progress monitoring to determine student response to instruction (Vaughn & Fuchs, 2003). In regards to application of an ecological decision-making framework, several implications are evident for assessment teams. No matter which assessment element is emphasized (universal screening, progress monitoring, diagnostic) these each must be reliable and valid as previously discussed. However, one other type of assessment validity to consider in an ecological framework is ecological validity.

Ecological Validity

The concept of ecological validity provides a practical grounding in interpreting and applying assessment results. Cohen (1995) described ecological validity in research as a practice that allows researchers to describe and evaluate "how real people operate in the real world" (Cohen, par. 2). In essence, ecological validity assists in ensuring that the assessment completed reflects real-world experiences while simultaneously yielding relevant results that can be generalized. Ecological validity in assessment provides a balance between the need to control for different variables (e.g., class size, academic levels, etc.) and the need to reflect the more natural environmental variables (i.e., classroom variances and differences), recognizing that in real-world settings some natural variables exist and may not be controlled within the overall assessment process. Consideration of the ecological factors previously discussed along with rigorous reliability and validity assist multi-tiered response to intervention assessment teams to implement ecologically valid RTI assessment as summarized in Table 3.3.

Table 3.3   Significance of Ecological Factors Within RTI Assessment for Struggling Learners

Ecological Element	Relevance Within RTI Assessment	Key RTI Assessment Question
Microsystem	The manner in which a learner perceives classroom experiences may affect assessment results.	To what extent does the learner value the classroom experiences and associated assessments?
Mesosystem	Learner experiences in the classroom interrelate with previous experiences and may affect assessment results as attitudes and perceptions change.	In what ways might one classroom task (e.g., oral reading) be affected by previous learning experiences and accounted for in the assessment process and results?
Exosystem	Influences of significant others in learners' lives may have profound effects on values, attitudes, and perceptions about learning and specifically the assessment of learning.	To what extent does the assessment team understand influences of others in a learner's life that may impact academic or social-emotional progress and associated monitoring of that progress?
Macrosystem	Development reflecting diversity in life may have important effects on students, which in turn, impacts classroom learning and assessment of that learning.	How might the assessment team relate cross-cultural development in the interpretation of assessment monitoring or diagnostic results?

(Continued)

Table 3.3 (Continued)

Ecological Element	Relevance Within RTI Assessment	Key RTI Assessment Question
Student Factors	Experiential background, preferred styles of learning, and prior education experiences affect classroom learning.	How are student factors considered in the overall assessment process?
Classroom Factors	Instructional expectations, learning time, motivation, or other related classroom variables affect student academic and social-emotional development.	To what extent have the different classroom variables been considered relative to progress monitoring or diagnostic assessment scores?
Home/ Community Factors	Parental and community values and norms shape the overall development of a learner, which in turn impacts classroom performance.	How have the values and norms taught to the learner been considered in the overall assessment process and in the interpretation of assessment scores?

As shown, implications for effective assessment, ecological validity, and associated decision making within an ecological framework are presented to assist RTI assessment teams to make informed and comprehensive instructional or diagnostic decisions. Each element associated with the ecological framework discussed in this chapter has direct significance to multi-tiered RTI assessment as illustrated by the sample questions provided in Table 3.3.

ECOLOGICAL ASSESSMENT FRAMEWORK IMPLICATIONS—CONCLUDING IDEAS

Hoover (2008) wrote that an ecological framework is not a new concept in education citing various authors (Carroll, 1963; Bronfenbrenner, 1995, 1979; Rhodes & Tracy, 1978), and consideration of the above discussed ecological factors provides important information to assist assessment teams to implement a valid and fair assessment for struggling learners in multi-tiered response to intervention. As stated by Brown (2004), consideration of ecological factors is essential since many issues, other than factors within students, frequently contribute to and shape academic and social-emotional needs found in today's classrooms. The following points summarize several tips for educators to address in their multi-tiered RTI assessment decision making. These are categorized within three primary areas and reflect the main ideas discussed to assist in the implementation of an ecologically relevant RTI assessment process.

Ecological Factors

- Three ecological factors (i.e., student, classroom, home/community) are adequately and meaningfully addressed in the assessment process.
- Four ecological systems (i.e., micro, meso, exo, macro) are considered relative to progress monitoring and/or diagnostic assessment results.

- Ecological validity must exist to best incorporate environmental influences in the interpretation of and inferences made from assessment scores.
- Progress-monitoring procedures are selected in consideration of the various ecological factors.

Educator Training and Preparation

- Teachers implementing tiered instruction receive adequate training and skills development to use research-based core curriculum.
- Teachers are well-trained in ongoing progress-monitoring procedures.
- Differentiated instruction must be appropriate to avoid misinterpreting learning needs as problems reflecting intrinsic disabilities.

Assessment Factors

- Assessment devices/practices are reliable and valid, and implemented with fidelity.
- Inferences made from assessment scores are valid for intended purposes.
- Assessment is fair and free from bias.

Form 3.1 provides a checklist for assisting teams to ensure that these critical assessment elements exist to successfully implement an ecologically responsive assessment process within multi-tiered response to intervention models.

SUMMARY

Implementing effective assessment in multi-tiered response to intervention requires consideration of a variety of environmental factors to best understand academic and social-emotional needs of struggling learners. This includes student, classroom, and home/community factors that influence development and progress in school. An ecological framework within which to implement multi-tiered response to intervention assessment provides educator teams the best opportunities to gather the most relevant data and make informed instructional and diagnostic decisions.

Applying Chapter 3 Learning Outcomes

1. Using Form 3.1, evaluate your school's efforts to incorporate student, classroom, and home/community factors into the assessment decision-making process.

2. Evaluate how assessment devices/practices consider an ecological structure (i.e., micro, meso, exo, macro) for struggling learners in your school, and demonstrate their ecological validity and fairness as used with the students.

3. Prepare and deliver a PowerPoint presentation to your school's faculty addressing the factors important to consider in ecological decision making.

4. Evaluate the ecological-responsiveness of your school's multi-tiered RTI model.

Form 3.1   Checklist for Ecologically Responsive Assessment Qualities

Instructions: Check each item that is evident in the assessment process.

ECOLOGICAL FACTORS

____ Three ecological factors (i.e., student, classroom, home/community) are adequately and meaningfully addressed in the assessment process.

____ Influences of four ecological systems (i.e., micro, meso, exo, macro) are considered in the interpretation of assessment results.

____ Ecological validity exists to best incorporate environmental influences in the interpretation of and inferences made from assessment scores.

____ Tier 2 progress-monitoring procedures are selected in consideration of the various ecological factors.

EDUCATOR TRAINING AND PREPARATION

____ Teachers implementing tiered instruction receive adequate training and skills development to use research-based core curriculum.

____ Teachers are well-trained in ongoing progress-monitoring procedures.

____ Differentiated instruction is appropriate to avoid misinterpreting learning differences as problems reflecting intrinsic disabilities.

ASSESSMENT FACTORS

____ Assessment devices and practices are reliable.

____ Assessment devices and practices are valid.

____ Assessment devices and practices are implemented with fidelity.

____ Inferences made from assessment scores are valid for intended purposes.

____ Assessment is fair and free from bias.

PART II

Implementing Effective Multi-Tiered RTI Assessment

Within the overall structure for successfully implementing multi-tiered response to intervention is the need to conduct various forms of assessment to closely monitor student progress. As discussed in Part I, these include: universal screening, ongoing progress monitoring, and diagnostic assessment for special education. In addition, each of these must be implemented in the manner in which they were designed and researched (i.e., fidelity). While the RTI process may vary across states, school districts, or schools, multi-tiered response to intervention assessment may eventually lead to special education eligibility decisions. Therefore, all aspects of the assessment process must be appropriately implemented and documented to ensure that the most effective decisions are made relative to struggling learners. This includes use of appropriate assessment practices and an understanding of the relationship between RTI assessment and special education. Part II of this book provides three chapters that address these critical assessment aspects within multi-tiered response to intervention.

Part II Chapters

4. Fidelity of Assessment

5. Evidence-Based Assessment and Assessment Accommodations

6. RTI Assessment and Special Education

4

Fidelity of Assessment

SIGNIFICANCE TO CONTEMPORARY ASSESSMENT

The proper implementation of evidence-based interventions and research-based curriculum, consistent with the manner in which they were developed and researched, is the foundation of multi-tiered instruction. This practice is referred to as implementation with "fidelity," and just as curriculum must be implemented with fidelity, so must the associated assessment. Fidelity of assessment has always been an issue in our schools and it becomes increasingly more significant in today's educational environment. The decisions made based on universal screening, progress monitoring, and diagnostic assessment for implementing tiered instruction, as well as possible special education referral, require the most effective application of assessment processes and practices to best meet needs of struggling learners.

CHAPTER OVERVIEW

Chapter 4 discusses the critical element of implementing assessment practices with integrity and fidelity. This chapter provides readers with methods for ensuring that assessment devices, practices, and use of scores are implemented with fidelity, consistent with the ways in which they were designed and researched. The manner in which fidelity relates to decision making in assessment is also presented.

┌───┐
Key Topics Addressed in Chapter

✦ Significance of Fidelity in Education

✦ Fidelity in Multi-Tiered Response to Intervention

✦ Fidelity in Implementing Assessment Devices and Practices

✦ Interrelationship Between Assessment Fidelity and Decision Making
└───┘

LEARNER OUTCOMES

Upon completion of Chapter 4, readers will

- acquire an understanding of the importance of fidelity when completing assessment within multi-tiered response to intervention
- acquire essential knowledge and skills to implement assessment with fidelity
- be able to articulate the significance of fidelity in the overall RTI assessment decision-making process
- be able to evaluate assessment practices and devices to ensure their implementation with fidelity

PERSONAL PERSPECTIVE

One educational area within which I regularly teach and provide assistance to educators is assessment. This includes both formal and informal diagnostic and instructional assessment for general class and special education students including those struggling in school. Among the many issues related to assessment, I have found that the proper implementation of assessment tests and procedures is often compromised. The reasons for this vary and include inadequate assessment training, insufficient time, lack of understanding of the assessment device, or inability to see the connection between what is taught and that which is assessed. My message to educators is that assessment integrity is essential to obtaining accurate and meaningful results. All too often, I have seen much time spent on assessment only to find that the instrument was improperly administered, administered in an area in school with many distractions, or otherwise unsuccessfully administered contributing to invalid results.

The implementation of assessment with integrity, and in the manner it is supposed to be administered (i.e., fidelity), provides us with a level of confidence essential to making informed decisions. My experiences have helped me understand that assessment implemented properly yields valid results leading to more effective instructional decisions. Given the significant emphasis placed on assessment within multi-tiered response to intervention, its proper implementation is critical. Additionally, we are all becoming more aware of the increased expectations placed on classroom teachers to regularly monitor and assess student progress. I have found that it is essential for teachers today to maximize use of time and be highly efficient in classroom management in order to meet these increased classroom assessment demands. I have also found that the ideas and suggestions provided in this chapter assisted me with assessment fidelity.

OVERVIEW OF FIDELITY IN EDUCATION

A fundamental underlying premise of multi-tiered response to intervention is that all students receive high-quality instruction using curricula, teaching strategies, and associated differentiations that are research-based and implemented in a manner consistent with the way in which they are designed and researched. Klingner, Sorrells, and Barrera (2007) wrote that tiered instruction must ensure that all students receive appropriate research-based curriculum. Therefore, the initial task in multi-tiered instruction is to ensure that teachers are using research-based curriculum and associated teaching and behavior management strategies with all students. However, the proper selection of these items is only one aspect of that which must occur to effectively implement tiered instruction.

Once proper selection has occurred, then proper implementation must exist. Selected research-based curricula, teaching strategies, and behavior management techniques must be implemented the way in which they were developed and researched for the particular population of students in the classroom or school (Klingner, Sorrells, & Barrera, 2007; Mellard & Johnson, 2008). This practice refers to "fidelity of implementation" and is essential to making informed decisions concerning the most productive level and duration of tiered instruction for all learners. In effect, multi-tiered response to intervention is initially concerned with the proper implementation of the research-based curricula prior to considering any decisions about the possibility of an intrinsic disorder within the learner. Should it be determined that implementation with "fidelity" did not occur, then the first course of action is to ensure this takes place to rule out the possibility that poor teaching, use of unapproved curricula, or other *instructional* related issues are not the primary reason that the student is struggling with learning. To best understand and determine fidelity, at least two factors must be considered—explicit implementation and hidden implementation.

Explicit Implementation

Explicit implementation refers to adhering to the stated proper steps, sequence, goals, objectives, materials, and time frame for implementing the curriculum (Eisner, 2002). For example, should the curriculum or strategy contain a five-step process to be implemented in sequential order and repeated daily for five days, then this must be followed to implement with fidelity. Should the teacher elect to skip one of the steps or go out of sequence, this method or curriculum has not been implemented with fidelity. While adhering to proper procedures for implementing research-based instruction forms a solid and necessary foundation, subtle ways in which these are presented may also have an effect on learners' progress.

Hidden Implementation

Hidden implementation refers to what actually occurs and is taught in schools that go beyond the explicit curriculum. It includes the result of "various approaches to teaching" (Eisner, 2002, p. 97) which in part reflects the daily decisions made such as the grouping of students or classroom arrangements—in attempts to implement the research-based curriculum or intervention based on actual needs of the students using it, as well as the ways in which each teacher "personalizes" the implementation.

The reality is, as educators, we are all different with different styles, preferences, and areas of emphasis in our teaching. Mellard and Johnson (2008) wrote that "Even with a solid research base, if teachers believe an approach will not be effective or if it is inconsistent with their teaching style, they will not implement it well" (p. 130). While all teachers may follow the explicitly-stated proper steps in the proper sequence, the manner in which these are delivered varies from teacher to teacher and classroom to classroom and must be considered when evaluating fidelity of implementation. For example, tone of voice, reiteration of instructions or key points, proximity to struggling learners, strategies for inclusive involvement of each learner in the class, time of day, prior preparation of both the teacher and students in using the required curriculum, or the overall classroom management structure may all vary across different classrooms even though each teacher is following the same explicit proper steps and procedures. These and related "hidden" elements affect the implementation of instruction as well as progress in learning and must be considered when evaluating fidelity of implementation (i.e., extent to which individual teacher styles, preferences, and management procedures interact with the explicit implementation of the curriculum or strategies).

Therefore, when considering fidelity, both the explicit and hidden aspects of the implementation of the curricula and associated interventions must be considered. This overview has been presented relative to the implementation of instruction due to its fundamental underlying importance in multi-tiered response to intervention. However, just as implementation of instruction must be conducted with fidelity, so must the implementation of all assessment found within multi-tiered response to intervention. This includes consideration of the concepts of explicit and hidden implementation of assessment and their effects on assessment decision making.

SIGNIFICANCE OF FIDELITY IN MULTI-TIERED RESPONSE TO INTERVENTION ASSESSMENT

The significance of fidelity in assessment within multi-tiered response to intervention is seen in three realities relative to making educational decisions in today's classrooms:

1. The primary basis for making decisions concerning the necessary tier of intervention is grounded in properly compiled assessment data.

2. The identification of struggling learners is made only after proper assessment has been completed and charted over time.

3. The potential for a referral and/or placement in special education is contingent upon progress monitoring and/or diagnostic assessment data.

As emphasized, the gathering, recording, and charting of assessment data provide the foundation for making critical decisions about struggling learners. Assessment in the form of universal screening, progress monitoring, or diagnostic is extensively used to determine Tier 1, 2, or 3 level of instruction for all students educated within multi-tiered response to intervention models. Given the tremendous reliance on these three forms of assessment, educators must make certain that each is conducted with fidelity in order to

- generate reliable and valid assessment scores
- be confident that the obtained assessment scores are as accurate as possible
- use the assessment scores to best help struggling learners
- best discern learning differences from learning disabilities
- accurately determine the best level or tier of instruction appropriate for all learners
- make the most informed decisions pertaining to possible learning disabilities

Most significantly, fidelity of implementation of assessment helps to avoid having learners be provided a tier or level of instruction only to discover that it was a misguided decision due to lack of proper selection and/or use of assessment devices and practices. Stated differently: *A high level of assessment fidelity relates directly to more accurate decisions concerning the best method of choice for level, duration, and intensity of instruction for all learners, particularly struggling learners.*

This relates to any assessment device used, assessment practice followed, as well as the decision-making process to determine the best use of the assessment scores or results.

FIDELITY IN THE IMPLEMENTATION OF ASSESSMENT DEVICES, PRACTICES, AND ACCOMMODATIONS

Chapter 5 of this book provides discussion of assessment devices and various assessment practices that may be used in multi-tiered assessment of instruction and response to intervention. As suggested, no matter which assessment devices or practices are selected and used, these must be implemented with fidelity. This section discusses various features and factors that are necessary to ensure fidelity of implementation in three important aspects within assessment: (1) assessment devices, (2) assessment practices, and (3) assessment accommodations.

Fidelity in Implementing Assessment Devices

All credible assessment devices possess evidence of high reliability and validity as discussed in Chapter 2. In order to implement assessment devices with fidelity, educators must be knowledgeable about several factors including

- population with whom the device was researched and developed,
- standardized procedures for properly administering and scoring the device,
- prerequisite administration skills of the administrator,
- recommended setting for administration, and
- time allotments necessary for proper administration.

Each of these factors must be understood in order to administer the assessment device with fidelity. However, knowledge of these assessment factors is only the initial step in the process; each of these must be adhered to during the actual administration of the device to ensure it yields the most accurate scores. Therefore, administrators of the assessment devices must be certain to follow all specified procedures, steps, and instructions and be prepared to discuss the administration with the multi-tiered response to intervention assessment teams. Just as teachers are now required to confirm that instruction is implemented with fidelity, so must administrators of assessment devices.

Fidelity in Implementing Assessment Practices

A variety of assessment practices can be used to further clarify educational needs of struggling learners such as analytic teaching, curriculum-based measurement, performance-based assessment, or task analysis. Similar to the implementation of assessment devices, every assessment practice must be implemented with fidelity to yield accurate results. Assessment practices are discussed in detail in Chapter 5; however, each contains suggested or prescribed steps, procedures, or guidelines to follow for proper implementation. For example, one assessment practice is *analytic teaching* and this procedure contains specific steps to follow. When implemented properly, this assessment practice provides valuable information concerning needs of struggling learners. Similar to the implementation assessment devices, the implementation of assessment practices must be completed with integrity. Additionally, evidence of that implementation should be documented and shared with multi-tiered assessment teams.

Fidelity in Implementing Assessment Accommodations

For some learners, *assessment accommodations* are necessary to gather the most accurate and meaningful information related to educational progress. Assessment accommodations are acceptable practices that assist in the implementation of fair and unbiased assessment. These include accommodations pertaining to time, setting, schedule, presentation of material, and response mode. It is important to keep in mind that assessment accommodations are designed to "alter conditions for assessment . . . which do not change the standards or benchmarks being assessed" (Hoover, Klingner et al., 2008, p. 135). Therefore, fidelity in the implementation of assessment accommodations must include ensuring that only the assessment conditions are manipulated and not that which is being assessed. Additional coverage of assessment accommodations is provided in Chapter 5.

PROFESSIONAL PRACTICES NECESSARY FOR ASSESSMENT FIDELITY

For many educators who are not assessment specialists, yet who are required to conduct assessments on a regular basis, training in assessment becomes an essential aspect in their professional development. In most undergraduate and graduate teacher preparation programs, educators are usually required to complete one or sometimes two classes on assessment. While other courses may address the topic of assessment, for the most part, the formal and detailed coverage of assessment devices, practices, appropriate uses as well as misuses, and biases is generally limited to one required assessment course involving approximately forty-five to sixty contact hours. In previous assessment models, a majority of individual comprehensive assessments were completed by assessment specialists (e.g., school psychologists), particularly as these related to special education diagnostic assessments.

However, in today's multi-tiered response to intervention models, all teachers are expected to conduct regular assessments in the form of universal screening, progress monitoring, and/or diagnostic. Today, for students educated in Tiers 1, 2, or 3, ongoing monitoring of progress is required to demonstrate student response to instruction. Thus, given the importance placed upon assessment scores in multi-tiered response to intervention decision-making—along with the limited amount of formal training and experience possessed by many who are expected to carry out these critical assessments—fidelity of assessment implementation becomes a highly significant concern. To address this concern, all educators involved in assessment within multi-tiered RTI must possess critical knowledge and skills such as those presented in Table 4.1. The table was developed from information found in several sources (Cohen & Spenciner, 2007; McMillan, 2001; Mellard & Johnson, 2008) and is not intended to be all inclusive; rather, some of the most critical areas are presented and the reader is referred to these sources for more comprehensive coverage of these assessment skills.

Table 4.1   Essential Knowledge and Skills Contributing to Assessment With Fidelity

Knowledge/Skill	Significance to Fidelity
Reliability	The magnitude of reliability provides confidence in expectations concerning consistency of scores over time, which is essential for making educational decisions.
Validity	Instrument's validity provides confidence that assessment scores are accurate, which is essential to making meaningful inferences or interpretations of those scores for instructional improvements.
Proper Procedures	Administrators of any assessment device or practice must be familiar with the stated and required procedures for proper administration. Failure to implement an assessment device or practice consistent with stated instructions may yield inaccurate scores leading to erroneous decisions.
Allowable Deviations	While valid and reliable assessment practices and devices will stipulate the prescribed manner in which each should be administered, many will also indicate acceptable deviations such as allowing the rereading of directions or providing probes and questions to elicit responses. Using allowable deviations often contributes to more accurate results. However, adding in other unallowable or unstated deviations contributes to inaccurate results, even if those results appear positive for the learner.
Acceptable Accommodations	Assessment may include the use of acceptable accommodations (time, procedures, setting, schedule, response) and these should be used with the learner if necessary to accommodate the assessment conditions. However, inappropriate use of accommodations may lead to skewed scores and reduce the assessment fidelity.
Prerequisite Language Proficiency	Any highly reliable and valid assessment device or practice should indicate whether and to what extent proficiency with the English language is required for successful completion. Tests in English for those who are not sufficiently proficient with English become nothing more than "English Tests" and cannot accurately test purported skills due to lack of language proficiency. Fidelity of assessment is contingent on knowing the extent to which one's ability to use English is required and then only using that device or practice if sufficient language proficiency is possessed by the learner.
Populations Used in Development	Assessment devices and practices are researched and developed using a defined population of learners and knowledge of this population is essential for their proper selection and use. Lack of knowledge about the population with whom the device/practice was developed may lead to inappropriate uses of the devices or practices, which impact fidelity.
Primary Intended Purpose(s)	Every assessment device or practice has stated intended purposes and recommended uses and these must be understood and respected to avoid conducting ineffective assessment. Fidelity in assessment begins with the proper selection of devices and practices reflective of their purported purposes and strengths.
Intended Uses of Scores	Fidelity of assessment includes the proper interpretations and uses of the obtained scores. Uses of scores from assessment devices or practices in ways not intended for use by their developers contributes significantly to lack of fidelity in assessment and should be avoided.

As shown, several key aspects associated with assessment must be understood and adhered to in order to ensure overall fidelity of assessment. It is important to keep in mind that these factors apply to any type of assessment whether they be formal, standardized instruments (e.g., Woodcock Johnson III); clearly defined and researched classroom-based assessment practices (e.g., curriculum-based measurement); or informal classroom-based assessments (e.g., teacher-made weekly reading comprehension test). Thus, no matter which type of assessment is implemented, each must be valid, conducted with integrity, generate results to be used in a manner consistent with the primary purpose of the assessment, and accurately reflect learner knowledge and skills. Also, as suggested above, if assessment accommodations are implemented, these must be completed in a manner that only adjusts conditions—not assessed knowledge or skills. Multi-tiered response to intervention assessment teams must ensure that all assessments used to make instructional decisions for struggling students have been completed with fidelity, which includes implementation by well-trained educators in the administration of universal screening, progress monitoring, and/or diagnostic assessment.

Fidelity in the Uses of Assessment Scores

Ultimately, fidelity of assessment is seen in the proper interpretation and uses of assessment results to make well-informed instructional or diagnostic decisions concerning the most appropriate level, intensity, and duration of instruction for all learners: *Assessment scores or results that are generated from an assessment process that lacks fidelity yield assessment decisions that in turn lack integrity, credibility, and value to those students for which critical decisions are being made in multi-tiered instruction.*

The need to ensure that assessment, similar to instruction, is completed with fidelity cannot be overstated and serves as the basis for accurate interpretation and use of all results, including but not limited to the following:

- assessment scores
- observational data
- curriculum-based generated data
- performance-based products
- work sample analysis
- task analysis

The topics about fidelity of assessment addressed in this chapter provide the foundation for completing rigorous, valid, and relevant multi-tiered response to intervention for all learners. Several of these issues and practices are discussed in greater detail in the remaining chapters of this book, which will provide more specifics concerning fidelity of implementation of assessment devices, practices, and uses of scores.

Evaluating Assessment Fidelity

As discussed, similar to processes that must be initiated to ensure that instruction is implemented with fidelity, so must these exist for ensuring fidelity of implementation of assessment. Form 4.1, Checklist for Fidelity of Assessment, provides a guide that multi-tiered response to intervention problem-solving teams may use to verify that conditions for assessment fidelity are adhered to by those conducting the assessments, along with important decisions associated with uses of the assessment results. This checklist should be completed for current assessment processes and practices to identify strengths and areas requiring additional development, to ensure that the most valid assessment be implemented with fidelity for all learners.

SUMMARY

The selection of appropriate assessment devices and practices is only the beginning of ensuring effective assessment for struggling learners in multi-tiered response to intervention models. The most appropriately selected assessment devices/practices will only yield valid results if these are implemented in a manner consistent with their development and research foundation (i.e., implementation with fidelity). The manner in which the assessment device or practice is completed indicates the extent to which the results are meaningful to make informed instructional or diagnostic decisions. Fidelity in all aspects of assessment is imperative if multi-tiered response to intervention is to be successful for all struggling learners.

Applying Chapter 4 Learning Outcomes

1. Discuss factors that must be included to ensure fidelity of implementation of assessment.

2. Select one of the main assessment types (universal screening, progress monitoring, diagnostic) and evaluate the fidelity of implementation of that assessment in your school.

3. Prepare and deliver a PowerPoint presentation to your school faculty on the topic of fidelity of assessment implementation in multi-tiered response to intervention.

4. Discuss the concepts of explicit and hidden implementation of assessment devices/practices and relate the significance of each of these to making valid assessment decisions.

Form 4.1   Checklist for Fidelity of Assessment

Name: _____

Type of Assessment: _____ Universal Screening _____ Progress Monitoring _____ Diagnostic

Instructions: Check each item after it has been confirmed within the assessment type completed.

Assessment Devices

____ Assessment was implemented as designed.

____ Assessment was implemented with students similar to researched population.

____ Manual/instructions clearly explains standard administration procedures.

____ Administration procedures were properly followed.

____ Examiner possesses sufficient background/training to administer device.

____ Proper scoring and interpretation of results occurred.

Assessment Practices

____ Assessment was implemented as designed.

____ Assessment is appropriate for use to meet students' assessment needs.

____ Assessment is appropriate for use to accommodate students' assessment needs.

____ Directions clearly specify standard administration procedures.

____ Administration procedures were properly followed.

____ Examiner possesses sufficient background/training to administer practice.

____ Proper scoring and interpretation of results occurred.

Assessment Accommodations (___ Yes ___ No—If Yes, check all that apply)

____ Time segments are adjusted.

____ Method of response is altered.

____ Setting or place to complete assessment is changed.

____ Manner in which assessment material is presented is modified.

____ Schedule for completing total assessment is adjusted.

____ Accommodations modified conditions and did not alter expectations/material assessed.

Evidence-Based Assessment and Assessment Accommodations

SIGNIFICANCE TO CONTEMPORARY ASSESSMENT

Within multi-tiered response to intervention, students are taught using research-based instructional methods, and the progress toward achievement of targeted curricular benchmarks or objectives is regularly monitored. An important assumption in this educational framework is that the assessment practices used to monitor progress (or make related assessment decisions) are also grounded in research and have been shown to be effective for the purposes for which they are used. Therefore, in addition to evidence-based interventions, educators must also use evidence-based assessment practices and procedures to monitor progress and evaluate student response to interventions in order to make informed and accurate decisions.

CHAPTER OVERVIEW

Chapter 5 provides competencies necessary to effectively select, implement, and evaluate evidence-based assessment to best determine learner responses to instruction. This chapter also includes discussion of a variety of assessment practices that may be used to effectively implement the three assessment types discussed in Part I of this book. In addition, evidence-based accommodations appropriate to provide an effective assessment structure for some learners are also presented, along with a discussion of gap analysis and rate of progress as related to RTI assessment.

Key Topics Addressed in Chapter

✦ Evidence-Based Assessment Process

✦ Evidence-Based Assessment Practices

✦ Curriculum-Based Measurement

✦ Performance-Based Assessment

✦ Task Analysis

✦ Assessment Accommodations

✦ Process for Interpreting Assessment Results

✦ Gap Analysis and Rate of Progress

LEARNER OUTCOMES

Upon completion of Chapter 5 readers will

- acquire knowledge and skills necessary to conduct evidence-based assessment, including gap analysis and interpreting rate of progress
- understand the important components in implementing curriculum-based measurement
- be knowledgeable of a variety of evidence-based assessment practices
- be able to implement appropriate assessment accommodations

PERSONAL PERSPECTIVE

Throughout my career, I have found that most—if not all—educators attempt to implement assessment that they believe to be effective. However, within this process, we are cautioned to avoid periodically and perhaps unknowingly deviating from the use of evidence-based practices within assessment. I have seen deviations in assessment occur primarily in several specific ways: (1) eliminating some steps in a defined process due to time constraints; (2) selecting elements from two or three methods and then creating an adapted, untested, alternate method for use in the classroom; (3) providing minor cues or assistance in an assessment that are not approved aspects of the standardized procedures; or (4) deviating from assessment procedures due to lack of proper training. These and similar actions, while completed in good faith, produce assessment practices that in effect are no longer evidence-based.

The significance of using evidence-based assessment practices is found in the need for reliable and valid results. As educators, we are reminded that evidence-based assessment practices, when implemented properly and for their researched intended purposes, provide the best opportunity for us to identify learners at risk and select proper evidence-based instructional interventions. My experiences in using the assessment practices described in this chapter have provided me valuable methods for linking classroom assessment with instruction as well as provide child study teams with authentic academic and social-emotional assessment results. I learned that by using these types of evidence-based assessment practices and applying the results to make instructional decisions, I was able to provide highly relevant education to struggling learners. Overall, the proper use of evidence-based assessment practices is essential to meeting multi-tiered response to intervention learning and behavior needs in the classroom.

WHAT IS EVIDENCE-BASED EDUCATION?

Evidence-based education includes the implementation of curricula, materials, teaching interventions, and assessment that are based on and validated through research. This specific book is focused on the selection, implementation, and utilization of aspects related to the overall assessment process within multi-tiered response to intervention. Therefore, while the issues and concepts discussed in this chapter are related to assessment, they also apply to other aspects of education (e.g., curricula, teaching interventions). Six guiding principles have been identified (National Research Council [NRC], 2002) that provide the foundation for determining research-based educational practices. These are presented in Table 5.1 with specific emphasis toward their use in assessment.

Table 5.1 Principles in Evidence-Based Assessment

Principles	Assessment Relevance
1. Significant assessment question(s) are investigated empirically.	Devices and practices in assessment are clarified and rigorously evaluated.
2. Assessment research is linked to relevant theory.	Current assessment research is connected to prior studies and research conclusions.
3. Assessment research methods directly investigate research question(s).	Quantitative and qualitative research is completed to respond to posed assessment research questions.
4. Coherent and explicit reasoning chain is provided.	Logical chain of reasoning to make informed educational decisions is developed and includes reliability, validity, fairness, and fidelity.
5. Findings can be replicated/generalized.	Validation of research findings across settings with similar populations is essential (i.e., ecological validity).
6. Results are disseminated.	Results are shared at conferences/workshops to add to existing body of knowledge.

Form 5.1, developed from discussions found in Baca and Cervantes (2004), Hoover (2009), and Klingner, Hoover, and Baca (2008), provides a guide for ensuring that selected assessment devices and practices contain evidence-based documentation.

SIGNIFICANCE OF EVIDENCE-BASED ASSESSMENT IN EDUCATION

The assessment of struggling learners often requires the use of multiple measures to best understand student needs. The use of only one measure or one assessment score may not provide sufficient information to make the most informed decision for instruction. Goh (2004) wrote that, in general, educators agree that educational decisions "should not be made relying on only a single measure or test score" (p. 14). In addition, the Individuals with Disabilities Education Act (IDEA) (2004) supports the notion that student progress or educational needs should not be determined using only one data source and that other assessment approaches should also be used including criterion-referenced measures, interviews, observations, or work sample analysis. Therefore, evidence-based assessment in multi-tiered response to intervention must include highly reliable and valid formal devices as well as other assessment practices such as those presented in this chapter.

Moran and Malott (2004) discuss evidence-based interventions and outline several items that reflect effective education. These items are not all-inclusive and are presented below, relative to assessment within RTI.

Assessment in multi-tiered response to intervention assists to

1. Clarify learner progress toward clearly defined standards/goals.

2. Determine if empirical models of instruction are used in the classroom (e.g., direct instruction).

3. Identify necessary differentiated instruction.

4. Determine progress toward mastery of content.

5. Ascertain the extent to which higher order thinking abilities are emphasized in teaching and learning.

6. Measure growth toward curricular benchmarks over time.

7. Provide connections among outcomes, instruction, and response to that instruction.

Multi-tiered RTI assessment teams must consider the research base when implementing each type of assessment (i.e., universal screening, progress monitoring, diagnostic). Valid assessment decisions often require use of multiple assessment results within a comprehensive process ensuring that the following exist:

1. Implementation of assessment has been completed with fidelity.

2. Assessment device has been validated for its intended use (e.g., oral reading fluency).

3. Selected evidence–based intervention has been validated with the population for which it is being used (e.g., struggling readers, English language learners).

4. Assessment accommodations occur when necessary.

5. Progress-monitoring devices and procedures directly relate to the curriculum being implemented.

6. Progress data are accurately recorded, charted, and interpreted.

7. Ecological validity is considered to ensure that diverse cultural values, norms, and experiential background are accounted for in the decision making.

8. Assessment device/practice was sufficiently researched with populations similar to those with whom it is used in multi-tiered response to intervention.

9. Multiple means to corroborate progress are included in the overall assessment process.

EVIDENCE-BASED ASSESSMENT DEVICES

There exist hundreds of devices used on a regular basis to assist with various aspects of assessment ranging from universal screening through diagnostic testing. In order to implement effective multi-tiered response to intervention, the selection and use of evidence-based and normed assessment devices must exist. While the specifics vary, several key aspects must be known to ensure that evidence-based assessment occurs when using any standardized device, as summarized in Table 5.2. The table was developed from information found in several assessment sources (Cohen & Spenciner, 2007; Hosp, Hosp, & Howell, 2007; McMillan, 2001) and each of these was previously discussed. The items in Table 5.2 are reiterated on the next page to emphasize their significance in the proper selection and use of assessment instruments with struggling learners.

While the use of normed and standardized assessment devices may receive less emphasis in schools today than in the past, if these are used educators must be aware of these important assessment characteristics to ensure proper evidence-based assessment occurs for all learners.

Table 5.2   Significant Factors in the Selection /Use of Norm-Reference Assessment Devices

Assessment Factor	Assessment Significance
Validity	Only valid device must be used.
Reliability	Consistent scores must be obtained.
Fairness	Use of unbiased device is essential.
Ecological Factors	Application to real-world settings is needed.
Intended Uses	Scores must be used for intended purposes.
Research Basis	Device must be grounded in research base.
Language Needs	English proficiency levels must be stated.
Fidelity	Device must be used and implemented in ways in which it was developed/designed to be used.
Population	Population the device was researched with is clearly articulated.

EVIDENCE-BASED ASSESSMENT PRACTICES

One of the more basic assessment components in multi-tiered response to intervention is the use of authentic, contextualized assessment practices to determine student progress toward specified benchmarks or objectives. An authentic emphasis provides educators with assessment data that directly relate to that which is being taught in the classroom, including its association to the evidence-based teaching interventions implemented. Several selected assessment practices are discussed in this section, providing assessment teams with valuable ecologically responsive information necessary to make informed, data-based instructional and/or diagnostic decisions. Of particular importance is that each assessment practice is discussed (1) relative to its significance in multi-tiered response to intervention, and (2) in terms of ways to ensure its implementation with fidelity.

We begin with discussion of one of the most widely used assessment practices to meet various assessment demands within multi-tiered response to intervention, including ongoing progress monitoring (i.e., curriculum-based measurement or CBM).

Note: The assessment practices discussed in the chapter include references to sources that provide more detailed coverage of the practices. A general overview of each practice is provided here for the purpose of describing assessment options to meet the comprehensive needs of struggling learners within multi-tiered response to intervention. For a more complete coverage of the selected practices the reader is referred to the sources cited in this section.

Curriculum-Based Measurement

Curriculum-based measurement (CBM) is an assessment practice that provides educators with "reliable, valid and efficient indicators of academic competence" (Fuchs & Fuchs, 2007, p. 31). CBM may be used for screening as well as progress monitoring over time. The following are characteristics of CBM, which makes this procedure a highly valuable assessment practice in multi-tiered instructional assessment (Deno, 1985; Fuchs & Fuchs, 2007; Hosp, Hosp, & Howell, 2007):

1. Students are tested on the curriculum material they have been directly taught.

2. CBM is research based with solid validity and reliability that clarifies a learner's level of proficiency as well as rate of progress toward benchmarks or objectives.

3. Criterion-referenced measures are utilized in CBM rather than norm referenced, making this practice more relevant to classroom and curricular contexts by assessing student progress toward achieving specific benchmark or performance levels and avoiding an emphasis on comparing student progress with other students.

4. The process for implementing CBM follows the same procedures when implemented both as a screening indicator and as repeated progress-monitoring indicators. This includes use of standard tasks, procedures, administration, and scoring procedures each time CBM is implemented, thus standardizing the assessment practice.

5. Academic and social-emotional behaviors assessed through CBM are clearly defined and counted within a specified period of time (e.g., one minute time frame) leading to a more objective documentation of that which is observed and recorded in an objective, data-based manner (i.e., number of words correctly read in a one-minute time frame).

6. Specific guidelines or "rules" are generated and used as a basis to determine adequate rate of progress for different learners who may demonstrate differing rates over time.

7. Since CBM includes a repeated measures design implemented over time following the same standard procedures (see item 4 above), it is a highly recommended practice for ongoing progress monitoring in any tier of intervention in multi-tiered instruction.

8. CBM is a highly efficient assessment practice both in implementation and communication. It is an easy process to implement once the standards are understood and it facilitates efficient communication of learner progress due to its documentation of frequency data reflecting actual performance recorded within brief segments of time (e.g., one-minute time frame).

Overall, curriculum-based measurement: (a) directly assesses that which has been taught, (b) records quantified performance data over time, (c) is completed quickly in a less time-consuming manner due to process of several short assessments implemented over time rather than one longer assessment completed at only one point in time, and (d) provides a structure for educators to acquire, record, chart, and share student performance data in standard ways so all involved may easily evaluate the quality of instruction provided and make necessary changes as indicated.

Implementation Process

As suggested above, the process for implementing CBM is relatively easy for teachers to complete on a repeated basis due to some simple standard procedures that are always followed. An example of CBM to monitor individual student progress with oral reading fluency was provided by Hosp, Hosp, and Howell (2007) and has been adapted below for our illustration purposes:

1. The teacher provides the learner with a grade-level passage of 200–300 words that represents reading skills that the student is expected to acquire and master over the course of the entire school year (e.g., select a passage from material that will be read near the end of that school year to ensure that the main reading skills from that year are included in the selection).

2. The same grade-level passage is placed on a teacher folder, clipboard or similar device.

3. The teacher situates self to clearly hear the reader while also ensuring that the learner cannot see the teacher recording the student response.

4. The following instructions are given to the reader: "When I say begin, I want you to read out loud this passage beginning with the first line, reading across the page (point to first line on student passage). If you do not know a word I will tell it to you. Do you have any questions? Please begin." (Start stopwatch and time for one minute.) *Note:* A different set of explicit instructions may be used or may accompany commercial devices; however, whichever instructions are used, these must be clear and understandable to the learner and the exact same instructions must be stated on all repeated assessments to monitor progress in this selected area of oral reading fluency.

5. As the learner reads aloud, the teacher follows along on the examiner passage and places a slash (/) through every word the student reads incorrectly or does not know.

6. After one minute of reading the teacher says "Thank you" to the reader to indicate that the student may stop reading.

7. The teacher places a double slash (//) behind the last word that the student reads or attempts to read.

8. The number of incorrectly read words is tabulated and subtracted from the total number of words to calculate the number of correctly read words during this assessment session.

9. The number of correctly read words is charted for this session and each successive CBM implementation to illustrate growth and progress with oral reading fluency over time.

Initially, performance data from this type of assessment activity may be used for screening (e.g., first three administrations) in which the average of the three scores is computed yielding the initial or baseline data point to be charted on a progress-monitoring chart for the learner. CBM data points are subsequently gathered with each administration and used as progress-monitoring results. Each subsequent data point is charted and interpreted based on level and rate of progress using the baseline data point and expected rate of progress as the foundation for decision making (the topic of rate of progress is discussed in a subsequent section). For each CBM administration with the same learner (i.e., one-minute oral reading fluency checks), a different yet equivalent passage should be used (i.e., equivalent reading level) and the identical instructions and procedures (i.e., Steps 1–8 above) are implemented.

The monitoring of oral reading fluency is one of the most widely assessed skills using CBM; however, this assessment practice is used for screening and monitoring performance in other areas as well. The above steps represent one example of the proper way to implement CBM and, for alternative procedures or additional examples, the reader is referred to Deno (1985), Fuchs and Fuchs (2007), Hosp, Hosp, and Howell (2007), and Mellard and Johnson (2008).

Strengths In Using Curriculum-Based Measurement In Multi-Tiered RTI

CBM has many highly useful purposes when incorporated into multi-tiered response to intervention assessment, including the following:

- directly assesses that which is taught
- assists problem solving teams to ascertain effectiveness of instruction
- yields data gathered over an extended period of time using equivalent material, yet following standard procedures for administration and scoring
- reflects progress toward mastery of a criterion rather than comparison to others
- is a quick and easy way to gather performance data
- monitors progress over time
- provides timely information concerning adjustments that may be needed in the instruction provided to the learner, including level or tier of intervention

Implementation With Fidelity

Curriculum-based measurement is a highly structured, easy to implement assessment practice that has the potential to yield extremely valuable progress data for individual and/or groups of learners. To implement CBM with fidelity, educators must adhere to the established standards and procedures each time a CBM assessment is completed. This includes use of equivalent material, identical instructions, same parameters (e.g., one-minute readings each time), as well as standard scoring procedures. When implemented with fidelity, CBM is a highly useful assessment practice within multi-tiered response to intervention. Form 5.2 (Checklist for Fidelity of Implementation of CBM) is provided as an example to confirm fidelity of use of CBM.

Analytic Teaching

Analytic teaching is an evidence-based assessment practice that provides educators a systematic structure to observe student progress and learning behaviors by subdividing tasks as necessary (Baca & Cervantes, 2004). Analytic teaching (also referred to as diagnostic-prescriptive teaching) is an assessment procedure that assists educators to evaluate effectiveness of instruction through use of objective data gathered from both the teacher and the student, relative to the completion of defined steps/procedures to complete a task. Collier and Thomas (1989) and Gacka (2006) summarized the prescriptive process followed in analytic teaching as including several key components: observation, planning, teaching, and modifications to instruction. An example of the steps for implementation of analytic teaching is provided below.

Implementation Process

1. Select activity that assesses the learner's needs related to suspected problem.

   Outcome Example: Student reads silently for one minute and responds to comprehension questions.

2. Engage student in activity (Step 1) and identify baseline performance.

   Outcome Example: Student is able to read twenty-five words per minute with 80 percent comprehension.

3. Building on Step 1, establish goal mutually agreed upon by student and teacher.

   Outcome Example: Goal is to be able to read forty words per minute with 90 percent comprehension.

4. Document the steps within an activity that student must complete to achieve goal.

   Outcome Example: Student and teacher will review key vocabulary words; student scans the passage to obtain main idea(s); student reads silently for one minute without pointing to words or lip reading; student responds to comprehension questions.

5. Develop two checklists containing steps that the learner follows—a teacher checklist and a self-analysis checklist for student.

   Outcome Example: Checklists should include main items identified in Step 4 (e.g., student reads without pointing to words; student scanned material and determines main idea; student correctly read required number of words).

6. Observe student completing instructional activity (Step 4); complete observation checklist while the learner completes the self-analysis

checklist; document on the checklists number of words read per minute and number of comprehension questions correctly answered.

Outcome Example: Both the student and teacher complete the checklists immediately after student completes task.

7. Review both completed checklists; determine extent to which instructional activity assisted learner to successfully complete the task, successfully respond to comprehension questions, and acquire associated knowledge/skills in the objective (Step 3) (e.g., read forty words per minute with 90 percent accuracy in comprehension).

Outcome Example: Results from both the teacher- and student-completed checklists are charted and compared; implications of results are discussed.

8. If necessary, select and implement a new strategy; observe and again complete checklists; check comprehension.

Outcome Example: Provide student with an index card to place under each line read to assist with minimizing pointing; complete task again and associated checklists.

9. Chart student's performance to monitor progress based on response to instructional activity and evaluate effectiveness of instruction.

Outcome Example: Student increased reading rate and increased comprehension after index card was introduced; continue implementing this strategy while observing, completing checklists, and charting results until goal (Step 3) has been achieved.

Strengths in Using Analytic Teaching in Multi-Tiered RTI

Analytic teaching provides multi-tier assessment teams with valuable information to make informed instructional decisions as it

- provides educators information about the manner in which learners complete instructional activities,
- documents student strengths and struggling areas in learning,
- assists in forming hypotheses of the student needs,
- identifies needed steps to successfully complete tasks,
- progress monitors student responses to instructional activities implemented,
- uses higher order thinking abilities that can be assessed,
- allows complex tasks to be more easily broken down for struggling learners,
- integrates instruction with assessment and monitoring of progress, and
- allows preferred styles of learning to be subsequently observed.

Implementation With Fidelity

When implemented properly and following the established steps, analytic teaching is an assessment practice that provides educators with a structured and systematic process for observing, documenting, and evaluating student abilities reflective of authentic evidence-based teaching. (See Form 5.3 Checklist for Fidelity of Implementation of Analytic Teaching.)

Interviews

Interviews are an effective assessment practice used to clarify a variety of student academic and social-emotional needs, strengths, behaviors, or preferences based on input from current and former teachers, parents, peers, as well as the students themselves. Hallahan, Lloyd, Kauffman, Weiss, and Martinez (2005) wrote that "skillful interviews can reveal much that is useful in planning for teaching" (pp. 79–80).

Implementation Process

To effectively implement a valid and reliable interview, the interviewer should use a checklist or form to guide questions and topics needed to be covered. Some specific guidelines to consider in the implementation of an interview include the following:

- Clarify the purpose of the interview.
- Document targeted questions or topics to address in the interview.
- Gather information on the same topic through use of a couple of different questions to make certain consistent responses on the same topic are provided by the interviewee.
- Assist interviewee to feel comfortable in the interview situation.
- Use the services of a translator or interpreter if necessary.
- Accurately record interviewee responses.

Educators should address the above items relative to the classroom situation and suspected area of need to further clarify students' response to instruction.

Strengths in Using Interviews in Multi-Tiered RTI

One of the goals of the assessment problem-solving team process is to best understand and interpret quantified data as progress monitoring is conducted within each tier of intervention. While quantified data provide the basis for response to instruction, for some learners, input from interviews conducted with significant individuals in the student's life may yield valuable and useful information to assist problem-solving teams to make more informed response to intervention decisions. Overall, information gathered from properly conducted interviews assists assessment teams to more accurately interpret academic and/or classroom behaviors that have been quantified through progress monitoring and/or diagnostic assessment.

Implementation With Fidelity

The fidelity of implementation of the interviewing assessment practice requires the educator to conduct the interview in a professional manner where the interviewee is relaxed and clearly understands the purpose of the interview. This is necessary to ensure that accurate information is provided by the interviewee, rather than responding in a manner the interviewee "thinks" he/she should respond. Honest and accurate responses are best provided when the interview situation is relaxed yet professional, and sophisticated educational jargon is avoided. Also, use of a few similar, yet different, questions to gather information on the same topic will increase the fidelity of implementation by yielding more valid responses.

Observations

Classroom observations assist assessment team members to corroborate other assessment results by providing direct observational evidence to support, refute, or further clarify assessment concerns. As formal, standardized assessment practices and devices provide necessary quantified data, the use of observational information assists to qualify that data in a manner that adds value to interpreting scores by considering various ecological factors such as those previously discussed in Chapter 3. In addition, observations assist to measure academic and/or social-emotional needs in a more objective, precise manner (Hallahan et al, 2005).

Implementation Process

Similar to interviews, use of observations should adhere to a few simple procedures to ensure validity of that which is observed (e.g., academic and/or social-emotional behaviors). These include ensuring the following:

- a clear purpose for the observation
- sufficient time to complete the observation
- observation of classroom task or activity where student must demonstrate skills or abilities (both strengths and areas of concern)
- use of a form or guide to document observed behaviors, skills, and related student performance abilities
- documentation of the classroom context and variables associated with the observed activity or task (i.e., antecedent and consequences to observed behavior)
- recording both the frequency and duration of observed behavior
- summarization of observation and tallying of frequency/duration data

Strengths in Using Observations in Multi-Tiered RTI

Alper, Ryndak, and Schloss (2001) suggested that observations provide important information in meeting assessment outcomes. Data from classroom observations provide problem-solving teams with valuable information concerning fidelity of implementation of the research-based curriculum and evidence-based interventions. Observational data provide information related to the context in which a student responds or fails to respond to core, supplemental, or intensive instruction. In addition, various ecological factors that may influence student progress may be identified through classroom observations.

Implementation With Fidelity

Observing in a structured manner, consistent with the documentation and recording of frequency and duration of exhibited behaviors, reflects meaningful observations of classroom performance. Fidelity of an observation may be confirmed by having a second educator also complete the observation using the same guide or checklist. The extent that documented results are similar reflect a more valid observation, thereby supporting fidelity of implementation.

Work Sample Analysis

Work sample analysis provides educators with specific examples, over time, of actual student work in targeted academic or behavioral areas. Work samples assist in assessing content knowledge and skills as well as uses of higher level thinking abilities (Goh, 2004). Using a rubric to quantify various aspects of student work provides additional information to support progress-monitoring efforts. As work sample analysis data are charted over time, along with other progress data, a more in-depth and complete picture of student work in various content/behavioral areas is illustrated.

Implementation Process

The process for conducting work sample analysis is easy to implement following four basic steps:

1. *Collection.* Samples of relevant work reflecting areas of suspected need are gathered.

2. *Analysis.* Using rubric or other quantified scoring device, the work sample is evaluated to determine evidence of desired qualities or elements.

3. *Charting of Results.* Data scores from the analysis rubric or scoring device are charted over time to illustrate trends in meeting desired outcomes in the gathered work samples.

4. *Summarization.* After a specific period of time has elapsed where a series of work samples have been analyzed and results charted, the student's progress should be summarized based on the charted data.

These procedures facilitate the effective collection and analysis of student progress as evidenced through work samples.

Strengths in Using Work Sample Analysis in Multi-Tiered RTI

Periodic analysis and charting of student work provides multi-tiered response to intervention teams with firsthand evidence of outcomes associated with specific evidence-based interventions implemented in the classroom. Actual work samples collected over time provide corroborating evidence reflective of response to instruction data gathered through other ongoing progress-monitoring practices. In addition, students may apply the rubric to their work samples as a value-added experience, particularly to use as a guide for becoming more knowledgeable of successful criteria to evaluate the work samples. Additionally, teacher and student scored rubrics provide insight into how a learner may have approached tasks reflected in the samples. Overall, work samples demonstrate authentic evidence of academic and/or behavioral abilities, and when put into a proper educational context, facilitate informed decision making to assist struggling learners.

Implementation With Fidelity

Work sample analysis must reflect meaningful tasks associated with the suspected area of need. Rubrics or scoring guides must be developed in such a way that they accurately reveal key elements (rather than superficial aspects) associated with the content or behavioral areas being addressed through the evidence-based curricula and associated interventions. Having two or three educators analyze and score the same work sample(s) using the same rubric or scoring device will help ensure fidelity of implementation as well as the validity of the work sample analysis results.

Task Analysis

Task analysis provides a process for identifying specific procedures and prerequisites necessary for task completion (Hallahan et al., 2005). When implemented properly, task analysis assists to identify skills a student has mastered and those requiring additional support in order to best complete a task. The sequential process associated with task analysis provides educators a structured framework within which multi-tiered response to instruction decisions may be made.

Implementation Process

Several steps should be followed to successfully use task analysis as an informative and useful assessment for instructional practice (Moran & Mallot, 2004):

1. *Identification.* The teacher initially identifies the specific skills or subskills a student needs in order to meet a targeted objective (e.g., increase vocabulary to improve reading fluency).

2. *Steps.* The teacher documents the discrete steps the learner should follow to achieve the objective.

3. *Introduction.* The student's prior knowledge about the topic addressed in the objective is activated by posing questions and generating discussion.

4. *Model.* The steps to be followed to achieve the targeted objective are modeled by the teacher through direct instruction.

5. *Guided Practice.* The learner is provided opportunity to practice the steps, with teacher support, to become familiar with the process to be followed.

6. *Student Feedback.* During and after guided practice, the students should orally describe what they are thinking and learning about as they complete the task.

7. *Independent Implementation.* Learner completes the tasks independently, demonstrating use of the desired skills and subskills necessary to achieve the objective following the steps previously practiced.

8. *Assessment Review.* During independent implementation, the teacher observes the learner and documents the extent to which the identified steps facilitated student learning of the desired objective; a short test or probe to determine acquisition of skills and subskills is completed and results charted.

Strengths in Using Task Analysis in Multi-Tiered RTI

Through task analysis, acquisition of a skill is systematically introduced in a manner that interrelates assessment with instruction (Alper, Ryndak, & Schloss, 2001). The implementation of task analysis therefore serves several important assessment-related purposes: (1) implementation of an evidence-based intervention occurs; (2) documenting the steps completed by the student, and its effect on achieving the desired objective, assists problem-solving teams to best interpret progress-monitoring data resulting from task completion; (3) the learner's ability to activate prior knowledge is ascertained; and (4) should the steps followed not lead to desired results, they may easily be modified based on charted data from brief probes completed to determine progress toward achieving and using desired skills (e.g., reading fluency skills). Through task analysis, educators break down learning in discrete ways, which assists to best ascertain extent to which sufficient progress is resulting from the appropriate implementation of this evidence-based intervention.

Implementation With Fidelity

The implementation of task analysis follows several defined steps to provide structure to the instructional task and associated progress monitoring. Adhering to the process within task analysis is essential if valid results are to be obtained. Each step must be implemented with integrity and the effects of the structured task on student achievement must be carefully monitored over time. Results should be charted to illustrate the effects of task analysis on student progress. Overall, if implemented properly, learner performance can easily be recorded during each step through observation and discussion, followed by short objective assessments (i.e., probes) to determine student progress toward achieving the desired objective targeted by the task analysis.

Performance-Based Assessment

Assessment where learner performance is evaluated based on a comprehensive student-constructed response or product is referred to as performance-based assessment (Bender, 2002). Significant flexibility exists in this form of assessment since the constructed product may take many forms such as a written project, poem, painting, essay, or audio/video tape. The length and depth of the constructed response also varies depending on the established criteria for evaluation and the desired outcomes for completing the product or response.

Generally, a scoring rubric is used to evaluate the product or response with quantified results that may be illustrated in chart or graph form.

Implementation Process

Successful implementation of performance-based assessment provides opportunity for educators to evaluate several interrelated elements that represent a comprehensive product or response (Hoover, Klingner et al., 2008; O'Malley & Pierce, 1996). This includes the following elements as illustrated in Figure 5.1.

Figure 5.1   Performance-Based Assessment Elements

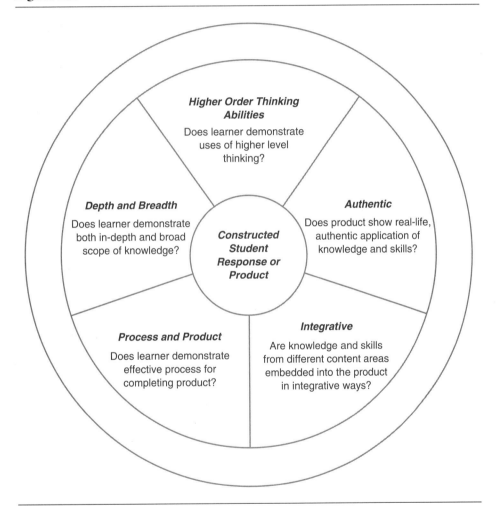

As shown, a comprehensive constructed response includes evidence of student use or application of (1) higher order thinking skills; (2) authenticity reflecting real-world issues, solutions, and application of skills; (3) integration of knowledge and skills across various areas (e.g., language, reading, problem solving); (4) strategies to generate the response or product (i.e., process) that reflect problem-solving abilities; and (5) response that reflects both breadth and depth of knowledge and application of desired skills. Additionally, Figure 5.1 contains questions to help clarify use of each important element in the student's constructed response.

Strengths in Using Performance-Based Assessment in Multi-Tiered RTI

Assessment teams may use a variety of assessment sources to make informed decisions about level and intensity of interventions needed for struggling learners within multi-tiered instruction. Performance-based assessment is another assessment practice that provides teams with a wealth of information to support progress-monitoring data, including extent to which learners use higher level thinking abilities, problem-solving skills, as well as application of knowledge and skills in authentic situations. Performance-based assessment allows teams to consider various ecological variables (Chapter 3) and their potential effects on student progress. In addition, this form of assessment provides evidence of skill proficiency relative to student-directed constructed responses that complements data generated from ongoing progress monitoring.

Implementation With Fidelity

Implementation of performance-based assessment requires educators to facilitate a learning environment that allows students flexibility to construct their own comprehensive responses or products incorporating the five major elements previously discussed. See Form 5.4 on page 90 for a checklist to determine implementation of performance-based assessment with fidelity.

Running Records

Running records is one form of miscue analysis for use with learners struggling with reading. It is easy to implement, and generates recorded data (Clay, 1993). Additionally, recorded results may be charted over time to illustrate student progress.

Implementation Process

The following steps facilitate the implementation of running records as described by Clay (1993) and O'Malley and Pierce (1996):

1. The teacher provides the learner with a reading passage written at the student's instructional level.

2. The student is instructed to read for ten consecutive minutes without interruption.

3. On a blank sheet of paper, the teacher records a checkmark for each word read correctly and writes the words the learner incorrectly reads *or* may put a slash (/) through each incorrectly read word on a teacher copy of the passage that the student is reading.

4. Omissions, additions, substitutions, and hesitations are considered miscues unless the learner self-corrects the miscue.

5. Chart the number of correctly read words within the ten-minute time frame each time a running record is completed to illustrate progress over time.

It is important to bear in mind that every word incorrectly read is considered a miscue unless the student self-corrects his or her error.

Strengths in Using Running Records in Multi-Tiered RTI

A running record provides problem-solving teams with authentic information about basic oral reading skills of struggling readers. This assessment practice provides a structured approach for educators to authentically assess student oral reading abilities when using both familiar as well as unfamiliar reading material. Additionally, when running records are completed over time, the charted data (i.e., number of correctly read words in a ten-minute block of time) illustrate student progress. This, in turn, allows running records data to corroborate results obtained from other oral reading assessment devices that may be used.

Implementation With Fidelity

The implementation of running records requires the educator to accurately record what is said as the learner reads aloud for a ten-minute block of time. Similar to some of the other assessment practices, use of a second recorder while the student reads will increase the validity of results. In addition, running records when implemented over a period of time (i.e., two school weeks), allow assessment teams to determine student progress using the same running record technique, which in turn reflects fidelity.

Functional Behavioral Assessment

The concept that behavior serves some meaningful function provides the foundation for understanding the assessment practice of functional behavioral assessment (FBA) (Durand & Carr, 1985; Webber & Plotts, 2008). More specifically, Crone and Horner (2003) wrote that "people act the way they do for a reason" (p. 11), and through FBA educators acquire a greater understanding of suspected behavioral problems or needs. Through functional behavioral assessment, the conditions associated with inappropriate behaviors are identified in order to develop a plan to reduce the occurrence of that behavior.

Implementation Process

Conducting a functional behavior assessment includes the implementation of several steps (Cohen & Spenciner, 2007; Crone and Horner, 2003):

1. *Conduct Interview(s)*. Clarify the suspected problem by interviewing significant people in student's life (e.g., parents/guardians, teachers, counselors, etc.).

2. *Conduct Observation(s)*. Conduct one or more observations in the setting(s) in which the problem behavior most occurs; make certain the antecedents and consequences to the behavior are observed and documented. Observations should occur over consecutive days and time periods (e.g., over a five-day time span).

3. *Generate Hypothesis.* Once the initial interviews and observations have been completed, generate: (1) an overview of the problem including antecedents/consequences, and (2) a hypothesis describing suspected explanations for the problem behavior, which in turn is tested as additional observations and/or interviews are conducted.

4. *Problem Solve.* Those most closely associated with the student (e.g., parents, teachers, counselor) and the problem behavior meet to problem solve by generating suggestions and procedures that may assist to change/reduce the problem behavior; ideas are recorded to be discussed further at a later time.

5. *Develop Behavior Support Plan.* Once the problem-solving session(s) is (are) complete, prioritize the suggested ideas and decide upon two–three ideas as initial efforts to address the problem behavior are clarified. Jointly create a behavior plan using the ideas agreed upon, making certain to document the following: (1) desired appropriate behavior, (2) conditions under which the desired behavior is most likely to occur, (3) possible reinforcers to be earned by the learner as the desired behavior is exhibited, (4) consequences to be implemented should the learner fail to exhibit the desired behavior, and (5) establish time line for implementing the plan.

6. *Monitor Progress.* Once the behavior plan has been developed, clarify an easy and quick way to monitor student progress by collecting/recording future observational data reflecting student's response to the plan; procedures for charting the data should also be established.

7. *Evaluate Progress.* Once the plan has been implemented for the specified period of time and progress data have been gathered and charted, review the student's progress toward exhibiting the desired behavior to determine effectiveness of the behavior plan; revise and implement as necessary.

Strengths in Using FBA in Multi-Tiered RTI

Functional behavioral assessment provides highly meaningful and relevant information to problem-solving teams in several ways:

1. Individual needs along with environmental factors are considered to best understand targeted behaviors.

2. FBA leads to the selection of behavioral interventions that are directly linked to the behaviors in question.

3. FBA is an evidence-based assessment practice that is supported by research (Crone & Horner, 2003; O'Neill et al., 1997).

Overall, FBA is significant in multi-tiered response to intervention due to its emphasis on observed behaviors and ecological factors that may contribute to the meaningful function of student behaviors.

Implementation With Fidelity

FBA includes use of interviews, direct observations, and review of student records to best understand student behaviors. Therefore, fidelity of implementation of FBA includes conducting valid interviews, targeted observations, as well as consideration of relevant information that may be found in the learner's educational records. Keeping in mind that behaviors serve some functional purpose when completing FBA, fidelity of implementation may best occur as behavioral antecedents and consequences are observed, documented, and charted over time. Form 5.5 on page 91 provides a checklist to confirm the implementation of FBA with fidelity.

INTERPRETING ASSESSMENT SCORES

As seen in the above discussions, these practices yield some form of assessment result, data point, or score. Some of the scores or data points are plotted on a chart to illustrate progress over time, while others reflect an aggregated body of work generated by the learner. Once assessment scores are gathered within RTI (i.e., universal screening, progress monitoring, diagnostic assessment) effective interpretation of those scores is necessary to provide the most appropriate tier of instruction. Two of the more important instructional decisions an assessment team must consider when dealing with assessment scores are: (1) extent to which a gap exists between expected and actual student performance, and (2) whether the learner is making an adequate rate of progress toward achievement of benchmarks or standards. The following are some suggested items to consider to best interpret assessment scores. These are not all-inclusive and others may be added; however, these are presented to guide assessment teams in assessment interpretation. We begin with an overview of the gap analysis and rate of progress aspects of assessment followed by suggestions for interpretation of scores. Suggestions were generated, in part, from sources previously cited in the presentation of the evidence-based assessment practices.

Gap Analysis

Directly related to determining RTI needs of struggling learners is the concept referred to as "gap analysis" in which the gap between expected and actual level of performance in the area of need is determined. The following steps illustrate the process (Colorado Department of Education [CDE], 2008; Shapiro, 2008):

1. Determine current level of performance.

2. Determine expected level of performance (i.e., curricular standard/benchmark).

3. Divide expected level by current level of performance. The result is the *gap*—a gap of over two is considered significant (CDE, 2008) as this size gap requires the struggling learner to maintain a highly aggressive rate of progress (e.g., two-three times) beyond the typical rate of progress expected of learners who are achieving at benchmark.

4. Determine *gain* needed to sufficiently close gap.

5. Identify expected rate of progress for students who achieve at benchmark (i.e., beginning of year benchmark minus end of year benchmark divided by number of school weeks yields the average weekly growth experienced by students who satisfactorily progress throughout the school year).

6. Identify time frame, intervention, and progress monitoring needed to close and assess progress toward closing the gap.

Consider the following example derived from information found in CDE (2008) for a student struggling in reading whose progress monitoring (completed at the end of the fall semester) yields the following data:

- current level of performance: 20 words per minute (wpm)
- current expected benchmark level: 68 wpm (fall term)
- gap: 68 divided by 20 = 3.4 (gap is significant/over 2)
- future expected benchmark level: 90 wpm by the next monitoring period (spring term/15 weeks of instruction)
- expected growth of those achieving benchmark: 90–68 = 22 wpm divided by 15 weeks = 1.46 wpm average weekly expected gain from those who make satisfactory progress
- gain needed to close gap by next monitoring period: 90 wpm minus 20 wpm (current level) = 70 wpm needed to close gap by the spring term
- intervention time frame: spring term is 15 weeks, so learner needs to make an average of 4.6 wpm weekly gain (70 divided by 15 = 4.6) to close the gap between the end of the fall and spring terms compared to an average weekly gain of 1.46 wpm for the typical learner who progresses satisfactorily during the same 15-week time period.

The next step in the "gap analysis" process is to determine the extent to which the needed average weekly gain (i.e., 4.6 wpm) is realistic and, if not, generate an alternate, more realistic time line. In our example, typical students making adequate progress will increase their words per minute by 22 (i.e., 90 minus 68) or a weekly average increase of 1.46 wpm, while our struggling learner must increase by 70 wpm (90 minus 20) or weekly gain of 4.6 wpm to close the gap by the next monitoring period of 15 weeks.

This expectation in growth over 15 weeks is highly aggressive for the struggling learner and a more realistic goal would be to have the learner achieve a 3 wpm gain per week rather than 4.6 wpm. This results in a 23-week intervention time frame rather the 15 weeks, which is derived from 3 divided into 70 = 23 weeks. The decision to adjust the intervention goal from a weekly average of 4.6 to 3 wpm is made by the assessment team based on knowledge and information about the particular learner and relative to expected gains from learners who make adequate weekly progress. Actual and expected performance should be charted on a regular basis to illustrate progress, in this instance, toward closing the gap between 20 and 90 wpm over a 23-week period. These "gap analysis" data serve to assist assessment teams to determine, in part, adequate rate of progress, need for adjustments to instruction, and the most appropriate tier of intervention.

Standards for Rate of Progress and Decision Rules

As previously discussed, in addition to evaluating student's actual performance relative to the established cut score (e.g., below 25th percentile) and the gap between actual and expected performance, the learner's rate of progress must be considered. Rate of progress for a struggling learner is determined by calculating the rate at which the student is making progress toward achieving the targeted benchmark, even though the actual level may be below expected standards/benchmarks. This result is compared to the average rate of progress expected of typical learners as illustrated in the above example.

To best understand and determine rate of progress (as well as "cut scores" and "gap analysis"), the specific type of educational standard from which actual and expected scores are compared must be known. Generally, rate of progress is determined by comparing actual scores to one of three types of established standards (Shapiro, 2008, 1996; Shinn, 1989; Wright, 2007):

Standard 1: Research Sample Norms. These are research-based norms derived from scores obtained from a research sample population. The scores reflect actual levels of performance in specified areas (e.g., reading fluency; written expression) as found within the research sample (e.g., average year-end reading fluency rates for specific grades; or, average weekly rates of increase of words read per minute for each grade).

Standard 2: Local School/District Norms. This includes reference to expected, typical scores as found within particular grade levels within a specific school or district (e.g., use of curriculum-based measurement to establish local norms in various academic or behavioral areas). These scores serve as norms based on results obtained from all students in a particular grade in the local individual classroom, school and/or district. Comparisons are made between local norms and current student-performance levels in the district or school.

Standard 3: Criterion-Referenced Benchmarks. This involves the establishment of minimum levels of mastery expected for specified skills and abilities (e.g., 80 percent accuracy expected in reading comprehension, written expression structures). These benchmarks often reflect proficiency based on rubric scores. Comparisons are made between a predetermined standard of mastery and current level of proficiency toward mastery of the benchmark.

Each type of standard used to determine rate of progress has its strengths and areas of concern. For example, *research-based norms* are convenient to use but may not reflect the demographics specific to the local population of struggling learners. The *local norms* perspective allows educators to more precisely demonstrate gaps in student progress as compared to other grade-level classmates. A potential concern, however, is that average scores may vary significantly across schools in the same district yielding unfair comparisons across district grade levels. Finally, the *criterion-referenced standard* reflects actual performance relative to a specified and predetermined mastery level necessary to best prepare students for future success in school (e.g., minimum second grade reading comprehension proficiency level necessary for success with reading comprehension in third grade). While criterion-based standards can be applied to a variety of areas in education, a primary concern is that these standards may be arbitrary and more subjective.

However, whichever standard is used to compare student's actual and expected proficiency along with determining rate of progress, each must be applied with fidelity to ensure validity and accurate use of results. This includes applying the "gap analysis" procedures previously described, to determine learner rate of progress as discussed below.

Calculating Rate of Progress Based on Research Norms. Growth rates are determined by comparing current student performance level with research sample norms reflecting: (1) expected level of proficiency based on grade/age peers, and/or (2) expected rate of progress within each grade as found in the research sample.

Calculating Rate of Progress Based on Local Norms. Growth rates are determined by comparing actual and expected levels of performance for each grade based on classroom, school, or district local norms developed through, for example, CBM (e.g., average third grader in the classroom, school, or district is able to read 60 wpm compared with struggling third grader who performs at 45 wpm).

Calculating Rate of Progress Based on Criterion-Reference Standard. Growth rates are determined by comparing current performance with a predetermined expected level of performance as set by a problem-solving team (e.g., 75 percent of written assignments meet minimum standards as determined by writing rubric).

Determining adequate rate of progress requires assessment teams to clearly outline the basis for making decisions (i.e., decision rules). This includes

- identifying the standard to which progress will be compared (i.e., research-based, local, criterion-referenced),
- determining the expected rate of progress for nonstruggling learners,
- applying the "gap analysis" formula to identify the magnitude of the gap a struggling learner exhibits, and
- applying these guidelines to accurately interpret assessment scores to determine rate of progress.

While decision rules may vary by schools or districts, it is essential that the guidelines used for making RTI assessment and intervention decisions be clearly understood by all involved. The importance of clear decision rules cannot be overstated: *That which constitutes a significant gap and insufficient rate of progress must be clearly delineated in RTI assessment, as these are used directly in making decisions concerning most appropriate tier of instruction as well as selection and adjustment of appropriate evidence-based interventions.*

As a result of their significance, use of cut scores, and the rate of progress and gap analysis procedures are aspects within RTI assessment that must be established by each school and/or district and subsequently adhered to by all assessment teams. For additional information about rate of progress and gap analysis, the reader is referred to sources cited in this section.

Interpreting Charted Data Points

Assessment practices such as CBM, analytic teaching, task analysis, FBA, or running records yield scores collected through completion of a series of short assessments or probes for the purpose of illustrating student progress over time (e.g., number of words read correctly in one hundred-word passage, oral reading fluency rate, progress toward meeting overall math benchmarks in a specific grade, number of times a behavior is exhibited within a specific time frame). These and similar skills are assessed on a periodic basis (i.e., monthly, weekly, twice per week) depending on student needs, and the results are plotted on a chart. These types of monitoring results may be interpreted in several ways:

- Actual level of proficiency is identified.
- Rate of progress is determined.
- Connections between what is taught and what is learned are made.
- Adjustments to instructional interventions are made, if necessary.
- Need for more intensive interventions is considered based on scores.
- Extent to which the learner is progressing compared to expected rate of progress is identified.
- Monthly, daily, or weekly progress is supported through illustrated data.

Overall, charted data assist educators to visually depict a representation of student progress over time, leading to the above types of assessment interpretations.

Interpreting Collective Pieces of Work

Some assessments include the collective set of abilities that culminate in a larger piece of work or result such as performance-based assessment, collective work sample analyses, or a series of interviews and observations. While each of these yield scores such as those obtained through use of a rubric, rating scale, or checklist, they often reflect aggregated aspects within the student's learning. These collective tasks are generally completed less frequently and yield progress toward several integrated skills (e.g., use of higher level thinking while demonstrating depth of knowledge, social and behavior management skills in different classroom settings, demonstrated use of several math skills through a series of work samples). While these and similar types of tasks may yield a lesser volume of assessment scores, they provide educators with insights into learner application of several interrelated skills within a broader context at strategic times within the school year. These types of monitoring results may be interpreted in several ways:

- Authentic application of skills and abilities are seen in student products.
- Collections of work samples may yield patterns of strengths or areas requiring additional support.
- Extent of learner's overall experiential background may become more apparent.
- An area of academic or social-emotional strength/concern is more thoroughly addressed and explored, including the role of ecological factors.
- Cultural and linguistic needs unique to the learner may be more easily recognized and supported in the classroom.

Different types of assessment practices provide a variety of important results requiring accurate interpretation as seen in these above examples. Whether the assessment practice yields a series of multiple scores charted over time or results that reflect a collective body of work, each provides multi-tiered assessment teams with valuable information about the struggling learner. Use of an integrated collection of assessment practices provides a more comprehensive overview of student needs, while simultaneously assisting multi-tiered teams to make the most informed response to intervention decisions possible for all learners. Determination of achievement gaps and rate of progress are also critical to accurately interpreting assessment scores over time.

ASSESSMENT ACCOMMODATIONS

For many learners, a variety of factors interfere with their ability to successfully demonstrate their true knowledge and skills in both formal and informal assessment. One ultimate goal of assessment (relative to instruction) is to determine the effects of instruction on student progress toward achieving curricular benchmarks or objectives. Assessment conditions that prevent learners from demonstrating their true abilities yield assessment results that are often invalid. Fortunately, several assessment accommodations exist that provide learners the best opportunity to demonstrate their knowledge and skills.

If necessary for struggling learners, modifications should be made to the assessment environment to provide a fair opportunity to demonstrate knowledge and skills. It is important to bear in mind that accommodations alter the conditions within which assessment occurs and not the goals or objectives of that assessment. Hoover, Klingner et al. (2008) wrote "accommodations are designed to alter conditions for assessment due to needs, which do not change the standards or benchmarks being assessed" (p. 155). To ensure valid assessment results for struggling learners, five accommodations illustrated in Figure 5.2 may be necessary to implement.

Figure 5.2   Assessment Accommodations

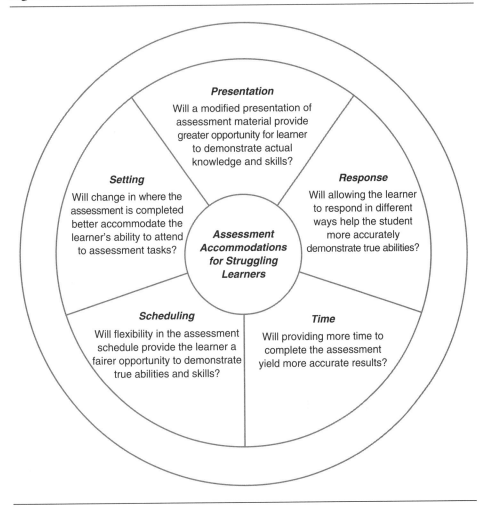

As illustrated, five factors warrant consideration for accommodation should the problem-solving assessment team determine that making modifications in one or more of these areas would yield more accurate assessment results. Specific accommodations may be made in the following ways (Hoover, Klingner et al., (2008); Thompson, 2004):

Presentation. The manner in which material is presented is modified, such as more or less reliance on visual or auditory presentation.

Response. The manner in which the student is required to respond to assessment items is altered.

Time. The time provided to allow the learner to respond to the assessment items is adjusted to allow for more accurate response.

Scheduling. In some instances, the test taking schedule should be altered such as breaking the test taking into different segments or at a more appropriate time of day.

Setting. The location in which the assessment is completed may need to be changed to a different classroom or other location in the school building (e.g., library).

Overall, the goal of progress monitoring is to determine how well a learner responds to instruction as determined on a periodic, regular basis. To be most effective, problem-solving teams must have a high level of confidence that the assessment situation yields the most accurate results to determine the most appropriate tier of intervention, and whether the evidence-based instruction is effective. Strategic and proper use of these five accommodations assists to ensure a high level of confidence in the screening, progress monitoring, and/or diagnostic results.

SUMMARY

Evidence-based practices provide the foundation for effective instruction as well as meaningful and relevant assessment. Today's assessment emphasis is placed on assessing progress toward that which has been taught and moving away from extensively assessing "deficits" within the learner. A variety of evidence-based practices exist and should be used to best determine learners' rate of progress, level of proficiency, and effectiveness of selected instructional strategies. Curriculum-based measurement is one of the most frequently used assessment practices to screen and monitor learner progress. In addition, several other assessment practices were presented in this chapter that add value to CBM and the overall multi-tiered RTI assessment process. These assessment practices contain established and researched procedures to follow to maintain integrity in their implementation, leading to more valid interpretations and uses of assessment results. The topics of gap analysis and rate of progress were also presented, complete with specific examples. The chapter concluded with discussions about assessment accommodations that are both acceptable and effective when used within the proper context for students who require modified conditions to best demonstrate their academic or social-emotional progress.

Applying Chapter 5 Learning Outcomes

1. Implement CBM with an individual learner, charting progress, determining gap and rate of progress, and present results to your multi-tiered assessment team.

2. Prepare a PowerPoint presentation illustrating the implementation of three of the assessment practices discussed in the chapter.

3. Design procedures to corroborate that each assessment practice is implemented with fidelity; implement the design for one of the practices.

4. Evaluate your school's use of assessment accommodations with students who require them and discuss ways to improve or expand their use as necessary within multi-tiered RTI assessment.

Form 5.1 Checklist for Evaluating Evidence-Based Documentation of Assessment Device/Practice

Instructions: Indicate whether evidence-based documentation exists for the selected assessment device or practice, and record relevant comments for each item. Summarize checklist upon completion.

Name of Assessment Device/Practice: _____

Does the evidence-based documentation for the assessment device/practice describe the following:

1. Purpose.   Yes   No
Comments:

2. Testing conditions/classrooms/settings.   Yes   No
Comments:

3. Populations included in the research and development.   Yes   No
Comments:

4. Effectiveness for intended uses.   Yes   No
Comments:

5. Classroom characteristics of those for whom device/practice was tested.   Yes   No
Comments:

6. Clearly defined school or field-based setting used to test/research the device/practice.   Yes   No
Comments:

7. Acceptable variations in implementation to meet diverse needs.   Yes   No
Comments:

8. Replicated uses of the device/practice in different educational settings.   Yes   No
Comments:

9. Summary of evidence indicating that device/practice is appropriate for its specified uses.   Yes   No
Comments:

Summary of evidence indicating selected assessment device or practice is appropriate for use with intended struggling learners:

Form 5.2 Checklist for Fidelity of Implementation of CBM

Student: _____ Date: _____ Teacher: _____

Instructions: Indicate implementation of each item in CBM to confirm its use in the instructional environment. Summarize checklist upon completion.

____ Students are tested on the curriculum material they have been directly taught.

____ Learner's level of proficiency as well as a rate of progress toward benchmarks or objectives is determined.

____ Criterion-referenced measures are used to assess student progress.

____ The same administration procedures are followed in repeated progress-monitoring assessment.

____ Standard tasks are used in repeated CBM assessment.

____ Identical scoring procedures are followed to score subsequent progress-monitoring tasks.

____ Objective data are generated for either academic and/or social-emotional behaviors.

____ Data are charted over time to illustrate progress.

____ Determination of "adequate rate of progress" follows specific established guidelines or "decision rules" and are consistently applied.

____ Actual classroom performance data are generated.

____ All CBM procedures are consistently implemented each time the same student or group of students is assessed.

Summary of fidelity of curriculum-based measurement:

Form 5.3   Checklist for Fidelity of Implementation of Analytic Teaching

Student: _____ Date: _____ Teacher: _____

Instructions: Indicate implementation of each item in Analytic Teaching to confirm its use in the instructional environment. Summarize checklist upon completion.

Specific Skill Area Emphasized: _____

_____ Current baseline ability/knowledge is documented.

_____ Appropriate evidence-based intervention is selected to be tested as method to assist student make adequate progress.

_____ All steps to be completed by student to successfully use intervention are documented.

_____ Process for monitoring student progress toward achieving skill/knowledge is developed (e.g., pre- and postassessment).

_____ A checklist listing proper sequence student must follow to complete the steps in using the intervention is constructed (both teacher and student checklists are developed).

_____ Learner completes the task following the steps outlined.

_____ Teacher observes student during task completion and records student performance relative to completion of defined steps in the content area/skill addressed.

_____ Upon task completion, student completes self-evaluation checklist.

_____ Upon task completion, teacher completes task evaluation checklist.

_____ Student's progress toward achieving desired skill is monitored and charted.

_____ Student's progress is compared to baseline data.

_____ If adequate progress is made, use of intervention and defined steps is continued.

OR

_____ If adequate progress is not made, instruction is adjusted (e.g., differentiations, alternate intervention), and steps for completion are revised.

_____ Revised steps are implemented and progress is re-evaluated adhering to the same procedures described above (i.e., complete checklists, monitor progress, chart results).

Summary of fidelity of analytic teaching:

Form 5.4   Checklist for Fidelity of Implementation of Performance-Based Assessment

Student: _____ Date: _____ Teacher: _____

Instructions: Check each item included in the learner's comprehensive constructed response. Summarize checklist upon completion.

Response includes evidence of student use or application of:

____ Higher order thinking skills (check all that are evident):

    ____ Comprehension

    ____ Analysis

    ____ Evaluation

    ____ Synthesis

____ Authenticity with evidence reflecting real world (check all that apply):

    ____ Issues

    ____ Solutions

    ____ Application of skills

____ Integration of knowledge and skills across various content areas (check all content areas that apply):

    ____ Language Arts

    ____ Writing

    ____ Reading

    ____ Mathematical Concepts

    ____ Science Concepts

    ____ Social Science

    ____ Arts

____ Response or product reflects (check all that apply):

    ____ Breadth of knowledge about topic

    ____ Breadth in variety of skills to demonstrate knowledge about topic

    ____ Depth of information demonstrating knowledge about topic

    ____ Depth in application of specific skills

Summary of fidelity of performance-based assessment:

Form 5.5   Checklist for Fidelity of Implementation of Functional Behavioral Assessment (FBA)

Student: _____ Date: _____ Teacher: _____

Instructions: Indicate implementation of each item in FBA to confirm its use in the instructional environment. Summarize checklist upon completion.

____ *Conduct Interview(s):* Clarify suspected problem through interviews.

____ *Conduct Observation(s):* Observe student exhibiting problem behavior over a several-day time span; record antecedents and consequences to the behavior.

____ *Generate Hypothesis:* Clarify the problem behavior and generate a hypothesis concerning suspected reasons for the behavior.

____ *Problem Solve:* Generate suggestions and procedures that may assist to change/reduce the problem behavior; record ideas.

____ *Develop Behavior Support Plan:* Jointly create a behavior plan documenting the following (check each as completed):

    ____ desired appropriate behavior

    ____ conditions under which the desired behavior is most likely to occur

    ____ possible reinforcers to be earned by the learner as the desired behavior is exhibited

    ____ consequences to be implemented should the learner fail to exhibit the desired behavior

    ____ timeline for implementing the plan

____ *Monitor Progress:* Clarify easy and quick way to monitor student progress by collecting/recording future observational data; chart data.

____ *Evaluate Progress:* Review student's progress toward exhibiting the desired behavior to determine effectiveness of the behavior plan; revise and implement as necessary.

Summary of fidelity of functional behavioral assessment:

6

RTI Assessment and Special Education

SIGNIFICANCE TO CONTEMPORARY ASSESSMENT

One of the realities for some struggling learners is the possibility of being referred for a full diagnostic assessment to determine eligibility as a special education student due to a disability. Should this occur, all rights, privileges, and due process procedures must be adhered to as stipulated in IDEA and other legislative mandates. Therefore, the overall process of multi-tiered response to intervention may eventually include consideration of many of the same special education factors we have been required to address over the past several decades. The significance of this within today's assessment parameters is that for some learners, differentiated instruction within Tiers 1 or 2 along with progress-monitoring data become synonymous with what was previously regarded as prereferral interventions. As a result, the period of time after a suspected learning or behavior problem is identified through the implementation of levels of intervention in attempts to address the needs of the struggling learner becomes significant relative to special education within RTI assessment.

CHAPTER OVERVIEW

Chapter 6 includes discussion of the connections between RTI assessment and special education referral and placement. Comprehensive RTI assessment is explored along with prereferral interventions to ensure appropriate evaluation for special education within multi-tiered models. The interrelationship among universal screening, progress monitoring, and diagnostic assessment for special education is also presented, along with the role of general and special educators in the assessment process.

Key Topics Addressed in Chapter

✦ Comprehensive Assessment in RTI

✦ Prereferral Aspects Within RTI

✦ Role of Multi-Tiered Assessment in Special Education

✦ Referral Process Within Response to Intervention

LEARNER OUTCOMES

Upon completion of Chapter 6, readers will:

- determine the interrelationship among RTI assessment practices in making diagnostic special education eligibility decisions
- be able to connect universal screening, progress monitoring, and diagnostic data to make informed special education assessment decisions
- acquire tools necessary to self-evaluate proficiency in key competency areas in RTI
- be knowledgeable of the roles that general and special educators must collaboratively assume throughout the entire RTI assessment process to support effective decision making for special education referral and/or placement

PERSONAL PERSPECTIVE

Perhaps one of the more controversial aspects associated with multi-tiered response to intervention is the use of this practice for determining learning disabilities. While the merits and concerns related to RTI and special education are discussed in this chapter, my experiences over time lead me to believe that however RTI eventually relates to special education, the same standards of excellence and due process within assessment must prevail. Results from a research project that I recently completed suggest that all states are, or will be, using RTI assessment results for special education decisions should a disability be suspected. Exactly how RTI relates to special education may vary; however, several basic assessment principles must remain. In my trainings, courses, and related work with today's educators, I stress the following pertaining to multi-tiered instructional models: (1) option for a special education referral and/or diagnostic assessment must remain open, (2) adjustments to instruction based on progress-monitoring results may eventually become prereferral interventions, and (3) however special education is viewed, it must focus on learner abilities with reduced emphasis on learner deficits.

(Continued)

(Continued)

One of the more encouraging RTI aspects embedded within the continuum of assessment in today's schools is that progress-monitoring results will provide a clearer picture of struggling students' needs. I have found that consideration of the topics covered in this chapter assists educators to put the strengths associated with previous special education prereferral, referral, diagnostic assessment, and decision making into the contemporary context of today's multi-tiered response to intervention models to best meet the needs of all learners.

INTERRELATIONSHIP BETWEEN RTI AND SPECIAL EDUCATION

While an underlying premise of multi-tiered response to intervention is to identify learning or behavior problems sooner (rather than later) in efforts to avoid the need for special education, some students possess disabilities that do require special services. In some instances, the significance of a disability is very apparent and the decision for formal referral to special education is rather straightforward. As you may recall, the expected percentage of students who may require more intensive interventions (i.e., Tier 3) to meet their significant needs is estimated at approximately 5 percent of the school-aged population. Also, as previously discussed, in some RTI systems, Tier 3 is special education (Mellard & Johnson, 2008), while others have suggested a four-tiered system where Tier 3 reflects more intensive interventions and Tier 4 becomes special education (Klingner & Edwards, 2006). However, whether special education is considered a Tier 3 or 4 set of services, *the fact is that a multi-tiered response to intervention system for some learners may include referral for special education; therefore interconnecting the RTI assessment process with special education procedures.*

Thus, RTI assessment results gathered in Tiers 1 and 2 provide valuable information should special education referral and placement be determined necessary. As such, this strongly supports the need and rationale for both general and special educators to be actively involved in the entire multi-tiered process to avoid previous situations where special education personnel "wait" for a learner to be unsuccessful with general education instruction and curriculum, and then becomes the responsibility of special educators who have little or no prior involvement in the struggling learner's education. Therefore, to best understand the interrelationship between RTI assessment and special education several key topics need to be addressed: prereferral and response to intervention; appropriate assessment opportunities in multi-tiered instruction; uses of screening, monitoring and diagnostic assessment results in special education decision making; and, assessment roles of general and special educators.

PREREFERRAL AND RESPONSE TO INTERVENTION

The practice of prereferral and implementing instructional interventions to address a struggling learner's needs prior to making a formal referral for special education has existed in our schools for decades. While initially the practice of prereferral intervention was an effort to differentiate instruction in the general class setting to address needs once they surfaced, for some it quickly became a cumbersome process in order to refer a struggling learner. In addition, the term itself implies that eventually a referral might be or will inevitably be made. Also, as diagnostic assessment increased in schools, the emphasis shifted from one of identifying needed differentiations/adaptations to one of looking at intrinsic disorders within the student.

Therefore, for many struggling learners, "prereferral intervention" became a required period of time where select interventions were attempted with some informal consideration of their effects documented over an extended time period to the point where the learner became so far behind that special education was considered the only viable option. This "wait to fail" scenario has affected thousands of students over the past several decades, leading to misplacement of many learners into special education. This practice also perpetuated a method that addressed struggling students' needs later rather than sooner in the process. However, as discussed in Chapter 1, this "wait to fail" practice should be reversed through multi-tiered response to intervention by identifying problems early and preventing them from becoming more significant through

1. early supplemental support.

2. ongoing progress monitoring.

3. instructional adjustments made as necessary.

4. continued monitoring and charting of progress.

As Vaughn (2003) indicated, students in multi-tiered instruction may eventually be referred for special education consideration, and Klingner and Bianco (2006) suggested that an underlying premise in RTI is that once students continue to fail to make adequate progress through extended applications of both supplemental (Tier 2) and intensive interventions (Tier 3) then an "intrinsic" disorder is presumed to be evident. As a result, for students who are eventually referred to special education within a multi-tiered system, the supplemental and intensive interventions become, in effect, prereferral interventions, with all RTI assessment results important in the special education eligibility decision-making process.

Prereferral and Instructional Adjustments

One of the more important aspects of multi-tiered response to intervention is the opportunity to adjust instruction, based on progress monitoring data, as soon as possible after indications that the student is not adequately responding to the instruction. This "adjustment to instruction," and associated effects of those adjustments, becomes a critical element in the overall multi-tiered instructional process. This is especially true for learners who are referred for a full special education diagnostic evaluation to determine eligibility for placement. Adjustments to tiered instruction illustrate attempts to address the problem prior to referral. Thus, for some students these "adjustments to instruction" become necessary prereferral interventions as required prior to referral for special education.

Prereferral and Continued Progress Monitoring

As instructional adjustments are selected and implemented across the tiers, continuous monitoring of student progress is required. For struggling learners, this progress monitoring begins in Tier 1 instruction when universal screening indicates a suspected problem and continues in subsequent tiers of intervention. As a result, over time, a significant amount of charted progress-monitoring data illustrating effects of instruction on student achievement and/or behavior are accumulated. Similar to the other aspects of assessment previously discussed, these data provide multi-tiered problem-solving teams with vital information about student progress when considerations for special education surface including the following:

- rate of progress and significance of gaps in learning
- level of proficiency
- effects of one or more evidence-based interventions
- needed intensity and duration of supplemental or intensive interventions
- appropriateness of special education referral resulting from persistent lack of progress

If persistent lack of progress is demonstrated after continuous monitoring, a formal referral to special education may be warranted. All RTI assessment information gathered thus far becomes essential prereferral intervention documentation that supports informed decision making concerning referral and/or eligibility for special education and the existence of a disability.

ASSESSMENT OPPORTUNITIES IN MULTI-TIERED INSTRUCTION

Multi-tiered RTI systems provide unique opportunities for educators to ensure that all students are provided sufficient opportunities to demonstrate learning through tiered interventions. In order for a special education placement to be made, educators must document that the student has had properly implemented and appropriate assessments within a research-based curriculum. Specifically, the following should be identified to determine sufficient opportunities with assessment (Hoover, Klingner et al., 2008):

- experiential background with the assessment
- proficiency in language of assessment
- student perception of relevancy of assessment (e.g., motivation)
- sufficient time to complete assessment tasks
- assessment accommodations (if necessary)
- relationship between that which is being assessed and that which was taught
- sufficient adjustments to instruction based on assessment data and results
- uses of valid assessment devices/practices relative to assessed areas

While not all-inclusive, these items reflect adequate assessment of student opportunities to demonstrate knowledge and skills within the overall assessment process. The extent to which these are not understood or reflected in the special education eligibility decision making is the extent to which the assessment scores or results may be invalid. Therefore, in addition to high-quality instruction, a major aspect within RTI assessment decision making is consideration of appropriate opportunities to demonstrate progress reflective of various skills such as prior experiences, English language proficiency, test taking abilities, or other related ecological factors that directly impact assessment scores or results.

APPLYING RTI ASSESSMENT RESULTS TO SPECIAL EDUCATION DECISION MAKING

As previously discussed, the assessment process within multi-tiered response to intervention follows a continuum where assessment activities become more frequent and more detailed as the learner moves across tiers of instruction. Should special education referral and eligibility decision making occur within the overall process, all aspects within the assessment continuum become essential. Below, in Table 6.1, is an overview of the process of using RTI assessment results in special education decision making. By responding to the types of questions listed in the table, vital information is gathered which eventually may become highly relevant to referral and/or placement decisions.

Table 6.1   Assessment Types and RTI Special Education Decision-Making Process

Type of Assessment	*Primary Purpose*	*Primary Question(s)—Is Learner . . .*
Universal Screening	Screen to determine proficiency in achieving benchmarks.	Above the established cut score? Demonstrating significant gap? Maintaining satisfactory progress toward achievement of benchmarks? In need of closer scrutiny for potential academic/behavior problems? Showing initial signs of struggling? Exhibiting the need for Tier 2 supplemental instructional support?
Progress Monitoring	Monitor student progress toward achievement of objectives or benchmarks on a more frequent basis.	Approaching benchmark cut scores? Closing expected and actual gap? Making an adequate rate of progress? Responding to supplemental instruction? In need of having additional instructional adjustments be made? Exhibiting the need for Tier 3 intensive interventions?

(Continued)

Table 6.1 *(Continued)*

Type of Assessment	*Primary Purpose*	*Primary Question(s)—Is Learner . . .*
Diagnostic	Pinpoint and clarify student needs, strengths, and areas of concern, especially if a disability is suspected.	Having specific needs met? Closing expected and actual gap? Exhibiting the need for continued intensive interventions? Responding to intensive interventions? In need of having instruction adjusted? Demonstrating intrinsic needs consistent with a disability? In need of a full comprehensive evaluation for possible special education services?

As shown, initial decisions pertain to meeting benchmarks that may quickly lead to more frequent progress monitoring. Should data suggest a continued lack of progress, the assessment decisions, in turn, move to making adjustments to instruction followed by continued progress monitoring. Decisions along the assessment continuum may eventually, for some learners, lead to Tier 3 intensive interventions and possibly the need for a comprehensive evaluation to determine eligibility for special education services.

Therefore, as RTI assessment is implemented and results are interpreted, a variety of questions are answered about the struggling learners' progress toward:

- achieving benchmarks
- making an adequate rate of progress
- reducing gap between actual and expected performance;
- responding to evidence-based interventions and research-based curriculum
- meeting individual learning or behavior needs

In addition, since progress-monitoring data may indicate a need for a referral to special education, both general and special educators must assume key roles in the overall process to best serve all struggling learners.

ASSESSMENT ROLES OF GENERAL AND SPECIAL EDUCATORS

One important notion critical to the successful implementation of a comprehensive multi-tiered response to intervention assessment system is the need for collaborative efforts between general and special educators throughout the entire process. This idea is supported by the Council for Exceptional Children (CEC), which wrote in its position paper that special educators should be active participants in the multi-tiered response to intervention process (Council for Exceptional

Children, 2008). As a result, both general and special educators assume important assessment roles within multi-tiered instruction as discussed below.

General Educator Assessment Roles

Multi-tiered instruction initially places significant assessment responsibilities on the general classroom teacher. These professionals are involved in both universal screening as well as initial progress monitoring for those who demonstrate at-risk levels of achievement based on universal screening results. Should a learner be provided supplemental Tier 2 support, more frequent progress monitoring will need to be conducted. In addition, in some school systems, general class educators may need to chart progress-monitoring data if this is not completed by others in the district or through a commercial organization.

Along with the completion of screening and/or progress monitoring, general class educators must also corroborate that they are indeed implementing evidence-based interventions and using these in the manner in which they were designed and researched (i.e., implementation with fidelity). Therefore, as can be seen, general educators are faced with adopting a classroom system that efficiently and effectively addresses the following minimum multi-tiered assessment aspects:

- incorporating progress monitoring into classroom instruction
- implementing quick and easily administered progress-monitoring assessments (i.e., probes)
- efficiently charting the progress-monitoring and/or screening results
- implementing a classroom management system that supports Tiers 1, 2 and 3 levels of instruction, along with associated monitoring of progress
- effectively documenting evidence for fidelity of implementation of assessment and instruction
- efficient management to incorporate additional time needed to conduct necessary multi-tiered RTI assessments
- using collaboration skills necessary to work with colleagues (e.g., special educators, school psychologists) to effectively and efficiently implement needed differentiations, adjustments to instruction, and associated progress-monitoring activities
- developing and implementing a personal professional development plan to acquire new or enhanced skills necessary to meet the general classroom demands associated with multi-tiered assessment

These and related skills and abilities are necessary for general educators to possess to successfully confront the time, management, curriculum, and monitoring associated with the assessment demands to meet the needs of struggling learners within a multi-tiered response to intervention model.

Special Educator Assessment Roles

The importance of active participation for special educators in the overall multi-tiered process is seen in the fact that a learner may eventually be referred to and/or placed in special education, along with the value in using their knowledge and expertise to help struggling learners and their teachers early in the process. Also as previously discussed, direct or indirect involvement of special educators is supported by CEC in all tiers of instruction. Several practical reasons exist for an ongoing special educator role across tiers, including the following:

- Consultative assistance is provided to general educators in identifying appropriate assessment accommodations.
- Opportunity exists for special educators to begin to acquire an understanding of the struggling learner early in the screening and monitoring process rather than waiting until the problem becomes more severe.
- Expertise with a variety of classroom management interventions can be shared, which may assist with the effective and efficient integration of instruction and progress monitoring.
- Collaborative efforts are undertaken in attempts to meet struggling learner needs identified through the classroom-based RTI assessments.

While the primary responsibility for implementing Tier 1 instruction and assessment rests with the general class educator, collaborative support from special educators often provides evidence-based ideas for differentiating instruction as well as for effectively monitoring progress. Support from special educators should also occur as Tier 2 instruction is designed and implemented. Active participation in Tier 2 provides special educators with valuable assessment insights into the struggling learner—insights necessary to complete meaningful and appropriate Tier 3 interventions should these become necessary. Also, special educator involvement in RTI assessment, either through collaborative consultation and/or direct support in Tiers 1, 2, and 3 provides assessment teams with valuable information and insights into the persistent needs of struggling learners including those who may have a disability.

Collaborative Roles in Assessment

Over the past several decades, much has been written about "ownership" of needs of struggling learners specifically related to general and special education. The reality in today's educational environments is that the school as a whole must respond to multi-tiered instructional needs of struggling learners using various supports and resources as needed. To this end, a variety of factors such as time constraints, professional preparation, experience, expertise, as well as common goals all require collaborative efforts to effectively implement universal screening, progress monitoring, and diagnostic assessments. Working in collaboration, assessment teams include various professionals with a wide range of expertise (e.g., speech/language, disabilities, assessment, diversity) necessary to successfully implement RTI assessment devices and practices.

In support of collaborative efforts, Hoover and Patton (2008) discussed five key roles within which general and special educators should possess skills in order to successfully implement multi-tiered instruction and assessments. The five roles, along with selected subskills are presented in Table 6.2.

Table 6.2   General and Special Educator Roles and Associated Subskills in Multi-Tiered Instruction

Role: Data-Driven Decision Making

Assessment and Intervention Subskills:

Curriculum-based measurement

Strategies for effective decision making

Data analysis

Multiple monitoring strategies

Basic skills assessment

Functional skills assessment

Special education eligibility process/criteria

Determination of difference vs. disability

Role: Evidence-Based Instruction

Assessment and Intervention Subskills:

Knowledge of evidence-based interventions in core disciplines

Higher order thinking skill strategies

Evidence-based instructional strategies

Task analysis/direct instruction

Analytic teaching

Understanding of impact of culture and language on learning

Compensatory strategies for students with disabilities

Functional living and transition skills

Mastery learning

Role: Social-Emotional and Behavioral Supports

Assessment and Intervention Subskills:

Classroom management

Behavior management

Applied behavioral analysis

Social skills instruction/assessment

Self-management skills instruction

Understanding of impact of culture and language on behavior

Social-emotional development

Functional behavioral assessment

Implementation of positive behavioral supports/behavioral plans

Role: Differentiating Instruction

Assessment and Intervention Subskills:

Accommodations and modifications for class management

Differentiation strategies in content areas

Second language acquisition

(Continued)

Table 6.2 (Continued)

Culturally relevant instruction

Sheltered instruction

Study skills and learning strategies

Student peer tutoring models

Targeted academic learning time (time, task focus, intensity)

Scheduling strategies

Alternative curriculum and materials

Adaptation to address functional living abilities

Role: Collaboration

Assessment and Intervention Subskills:

Communication skills

Coteaching/team processes

Consulting/coaching

Change strategies

Parent-school-community partnerships

Cultural/linguistic diversity and collaboration

Work with parents on IEP and disability related issues

Knowledge/understanding of IDEA

Knowledge of district special education referral and assessment process

Source: Hoover & Patton, 2008. Adapted with permission.

While none of these roles or subskills are new in education and not all-inclusive, these represent critical aspects needed to meet the increased instructional and assessment demands in today's contemporary instructional environments. As educators become more proficient with each role, proficiency with overall assessment will also increase due to the interrelationship between instruction and assessment. Form 6.1 provides a self-evaluation tool to assist general and special educators to determine their strengths regarding proficiency with each role. Results from this informal scale may assist educators to develop professional development plans targeting desired role(s) to increase assessment expertise in multi-tiered response to intervention.

SUMMARY

The fact that some learners will be placed into special education at some point in the multi-tiered response to intervention model clearly demonstrates that it is a process that must involve both general and special educators. The multi-tiered process, for those struggling learners who are eventually referred for a comprehensive diagnostic assessment, becomes a process where a variety of prereferral-type activities are completed, evaluated, adjusted, and determined to be insufficient to allow the student to continue to make adequate progress. As emphasized in this chapter, while an ultimate goal of multi-tiered response to intervention is to reduce the need for special education, the reality is for some students this becomes necessary and warranted. Due to the interconnectedness of RTI assessment and potential special education placement, both general and special educators need to be actively involved to assist, either directly or indirectly, in the overall RTI assessment process.

Applying Chapter 6 Learning Outcomes

1. Evaluate the roles of general and special educators in the multi-tiered RTI process in your school to determine if their expertise is being utilized wisely.

2. Conduct a school-wide evaluation of collaborative support for RTI assessment that general educators desire, and identify ways to provide this support.

3. Determine how your school's multi-tiered model facilitates the implementation of RTI assessment efforts prior to making a formal referral to special education.

4. Develop a PowerPoint presentation describing the continuum of assessment in your school illustrating how RTI assessment and a possible special education placement are interconnected and present this to colleagues.

Form 6.1   Checklist for Self-Evaluation of General and Special Educator Roles in Multi-Tiered Instruction

Instructions: Place a check next to each subskill in which you have proficiency in implementing. Items left blank reflect areas requiring additional professional development. Provide a short summary for each section.

I. Data-Driven Decision Making

____ Curriculum-based measurement

____ Strategies for effective decision making

____ Data analysis

____ Multiple monitoring strategies

____ Basic skills assessment

____ Functional skills assessment

____ Special education eligibility process/criteria

____ Determination of difference vs. disability

Summary of current proficiency with data-driven decision making:

II. Evidence-Based Instruction

____ Knowledge of evidence based interventions in core disciplines

____ Higher-order thinking skill strategies

____ Task analysis

____ Direct instruction

____ Analytic teaching

____ Understanding of impact of culture and language on learning

____ Compensatory strategies for students with disabilities

____ Functional living skills

____ Transition skills

____ Mastery learning

Summary of current proficiency with evidence-based interventions:

III. Social-Emotional and Behavioral Supports

___ Classroom management

___ Behavior management

___ Applied behavioral analysis

___ Social skills instruction/assessment

___ Self-management skills instruction

___ Understanding of impact of culture and language on behavior

___ Social-emotional development

___ Functional behavioral assessment

___ Positive behavioral supports

___ Implementation of behavioral intervention plans

Summary of current proficiency with social-emotional and behavioral supports:

IV. Differentiating Instruction

___ Accommodations and modifications for class management

___ Differentiation strategies for content areas

___ Second language acquisition

___ Culturally relevant instruction

___ Sheltered instruction

___ Study skills and learning strategies

___Student peer tutoring models

___ Targeted academic learning time (time, task focus, intensity)

___ Scheduling strategies

___ Alternative curriculum and materials

___ Adaptation to address functional living abilities

Summary of current proficiency with differentiating instruction:

(Continued)

Form 6.1 (Continued)

V. Collaboration

___ Communication skills

___ Coteaching/team processes

___ Consulting/coaching

___ Change strategies

___ Parent-school-community partnerships

___ Cultural/linguistic diversity and collaboration

___ Work with parents on IEP and disability related issues

___ Knowledge/understanding of IDEA

___ Knowledge of district special education referral and assessment process

Summary of current proficiency with collaboration:

Source: Hoover & Patton, 2005. Adapted with Permission.

PART III

Making Effective Multi-Tiered RTI Assessment Decisions

Assessment within multi-tiered response to intervention has two major components: gathering data and using that data to make informed decisions. Part II discussed the various methods and processes used to gather data. Part III provides three chapters that discuss the decision-making process to best use that data to meet the needs of struggling and at-risk learners. Topics include presentation of a model designed to assist assessment teams to make informed decisions, while considering various ecological factors previously presented. In addition, specific issues necessary to consider when implementing RTI with diverse learners are discussed. Skills and practices of multi-tiered assessment teams are also discussed to best ensure the most effective assessment decision making for all students. Part III and the book conclude with discussions of future assessment challenges as multi-tiered response to intervention becomes more widespread in our schools.

Part III Chapters

7. Assessment Decision-Making Process in Multi-Tiered RTI

8. Distinguishing Learning Differences From Disabilities Through RTI Assessment

9. Future Challenges in RTI Assessment

7

Assessment Decision-Making Process in Multi-Tiered RTI

SIGNIFICANCE TO CONTEMPORARY ASSESSMENT

The importance of an effective process for making informed and responsive decisions about levels of intervention, fidelity of implementation, and monitored progress cannot be overstated in multi-tiered response to intervention. Relevant decisions about learner needs require an organized and systemic decision-making process to ensure that necessary information is considered by the decision-making team. Concerns that use of the same interventions or assessment practices for all students highlights the many diversity issues that challenge problem-solving teams, emphasizing the notion that one size, intervention, or assessment practice does not fit all needs. As a result, an effective problem-solving process in multi-tiered assessment is essential to adequately address various levels of response to intervention exhibited by students struggling in today's classrooms.

CHAPTER OVERVIEW

Chapter 7 includes discussion of a team process and the roles that various team members must assume to best implement effective decisions within multi-tiered response to intervention. Also discussed are steps to follow within the combined standard treatment-problem-solving model introduced in Part I. Strategies for evaluating the effectiveness of the decision-making process and associated decisions are also presented, along with checklists for ensuring that team members provide input based on areas of expertise as well as successfully implement the combined standard treatment problem-solving model.

Key Topics Addressed in Chapter

✦ Team Decision-Making Process

✦ Combined Standard Treatment Problem-Solving Model

✦ Assessment/Decision-Making Team Members and Roles

✦ Process to Implement Standard Treatment Problem-Solving Model

---

LEARNER OUTCOMES

Upon completion of Chapter 7, readers will

- articulate the steps in a standard treatment problem-solving model
- be able to implement individual roles in the problem-solving decision-making process
- acquire skills necessary to evaluate the effectiveness of the problem-solving decision-making process
- be able to evaluate the effectiveness of the team decisions

---

PERSONAL PERSPECTIVE

In my work with today's educators and school systems, I find that many schools are converting their existing teacher-assistance teams or child-study teams to fulfill the role of a RTI decision-making team. This transition appears to be occurring rather smoothly; however, some concerns have surfaced. Within this transition, I have found the following to be of benefit to the teams: (1) ensure that the team recognizes that the primary role of the RTI team is now one of prevention rather than assessment and diagnosis; (2) be certain to remain open to the fact that additional team members may be needed on the RTI team; (3) recognize, as team members, that providing support to colleagues in making instructional decisions and progress monitoring is an important part of the team's role; and (4) ensure that the team process is clearly understood and adhered to by all members.

These practices will assist teams to more clearly articulate member roles and responsibilities, which in turn, will reflect the quality of the decision-making process. Some additional considerations that I believe important in the decision-making process are that of documenting decisions, recording the support to be

(Continued)

(Continued)

provided to general class educators related to progress monitoring, establishing future meeting times to be held to further discuss the student's progress, as well as periodically self-evaluating the team's process and results. The information found in this chapter has provided me with a sound structure reflecting my work on problem-solving teams as well as assisting others to develop and implement their teams. My work as a teacher, supervisor, and university instructor over the past few decades has reinforced the importance of an effective decision-making process such as the example provided in this chapter.

TEAM DECISION-MAKING PROCESS

Fundamental to multi-tiered response to intervention is the process for making informed data-based decisions concerning the most appropriate level of instruction for struggling learners. As presented in Chapter 1, most school systems are using or planning to use a three-tiered instructional framework to provide increasingly more intensive interventions should progress monitoring indicate that instructional need. To best make these important decisions many school systems use a process referred to as the standard treatment problem-solving model, where aspects of two different models within response to intervention are blended to provide a more complete assessment decision-making process for struggling learners. These models were previously presented in Chapter 1 and the reader is referred to Table 1.2 for a review of each decision-making model.

Our focus in this chapter is on team membership and associated roles necessary to make a combined standard treatment problem-solving model function most efficiently and effectively. While the process and aspects associated with a standard treatment problem-solving model will vary across school systems, some fundamental, key elements exist forming a solid team foundation. We begin our discussions with an overview of the key personnel that should be included on a standard treatment problem-solving team followed by discussion of an example of a team process for effective decision making.

STANDARD TREATMENT PROBLEM-SOLVING TEAM MEMBERSHIP

Several key and related personnel are necessary to make the combined model most effective for multi-tiered assessment. These roles are presented in Table 7.1 followed by a more detailed description of specific contributions to the teams.

Table 7.1   Key and Related Personnel on Standard Treatment Problem-Solving Teams

Key Personnel (Should be included on all teams)	Significance to Multi-Tiered Assessment Teams
General Class Teacher	Provides direct instruction to struggling learners; gathers/presents progress-monitoring data in Tiers 1 and/or 2
Special Educator	Provides special education expertise relative to all tiers of intervention
Assessment Specialist	Provides expertise/support for all aspects of tiered assessments (universal screening, progress monitoring, diagnostic)
Content Area Specialist/Interventionist	Provides content area expertise for struggling learners in all tiers of intervention (e.g., reading, math)
Parents/Guardians	Provide valuable input concerning home or community issues related to needs of student, particularly for diverse learners
Related Significant Personnel (Should be included based on student needs)	Significance to Multi-Tiered Assessment Teams
Bilingual/ESL Teacher	Provides bilingual/ESL expertise for diverse learners in all tiers of intervention
Speech/Language Specialist	Provides speech/language expertise including assistance to determine language difference from language disorders in all tiers of intervention
Behavioral Specialist/Interventionist	Provides expertise in social-emotional and related behavior needs (e.g., positive behavior supports)
Paraprofessional	Provides firsthand accounts of experiences through direct work with struggling learners

As shown, several educators and related personnel should be an integral part of every multi-tiered RTI assessment team, along with other selected members based on particular student needs. It is important to note that, to secure necessary information and expertise, input from any related person to the team should be solicited even if the individual is not a regular attending member. Each member assumes a significant role as detailed below.

General Class Teacher

The initial tier of intervention rests upon the skills and abilities of the general class teacher to implement research-based curriculum and proven instructional interventions. Once identified through universal screening, struggling learners provide specific challenges to general educators. As a result, the classroom data along with input and insights of the general class educator are critical to the RTI team decision-making process. This includes the general educators' abilities to share student work samples, progress-monitoring data, evidence of differentiated instruction and associated results, insight into specific student needs and preferences toward learning, or other related findings associated with classroom observations and interviews of the student relative to the area of need.

Special Educator

As discussed in the previous chapter, the reality within multi-tiered instruction is that some students may eventually be referred and/or placed into special education. Students who are determined to have a disability within the third level of intervention, for the most part, will have had their disability throughout the entire multi-tiered process beginning in Tier 1 and continuing through Tier 2 instruction. As a result, special educators have a critical role in the entire multi-tiered process especially through representation on the standard treatment problem-solving teams. Specifically, special educators are essential members of teams due to their abilities to: (1) provide expertise in disability needs, (2) interpret student progress-monitoring data relative to suspected disabilities, (3) suggest necessary assessment accommodations, and (4) lead discussions that clarify differences between intrinsic disorders and insufficient instruction. In addition, special educators may ensure that a proper referral to special education occurs should lack of response to instruction suggest the need for more intensive, specialized education.

Assessment Specialist

As discussed throughout this book, the assessment process, scores, and uses of the results are fundamental to making multi-tiered instructional decisions. Therefore, every multi-tiered RTI team must include an educator with assessment expertise. Specifically, this member may include the school psychologist or diagnostician who should be able to provide the team with expertise in a variety of assessment-related areas including universal screening, progress monitoring, diagnostic testing, validity, fairness, fidelity, and reliability. Ability to clarify specifics concerning evidence-based assessment and interventions is also necessary.

Content Area Specialist

Given that most learners who struggle in school have problems with one or more academic areas, the services of a content area specialist or interventionist specific to the academic need should be part of each standard treatment problem-solving team. Since reading is the most prevalent area of need, this discussion focuses on that content area. However, each of these points provided for reading can easily be applied to other content areas. The content area reading specialist provides knowledge and expertise to the team in the development and scope and sequence of reading—including development in the main areas of phonemic awareness, fluency, oral/silent reading, phonics, vocabulary, and comprehension. The specialist may also assist the team to pinpoint the students' strengths and weaknesses in reading, clarifying necessary reading objectives, identifying evidence-based reading interventions, as well as recommending needed Tier 2/3 supplemental or intensive support. Additionally, the reading specialist may assist with the collection of and/or interpretation of progress-monitoring data to make the most informed decisions concerning the most appropriate level and intensity of reading support.

Bilingual/ESL Teacher

If the struggling student is an English language learner (ELL), then the problem-solving team must include participation from a bilingual/ESL educator. This member will provide necessary cultural and linguistic support to the team by advocating for the needs of ELLs. This includes needs and issues related to culturally relevant response to intervention (e.g., acculturation, second language acquisition, difference versus disability). A bilingual/ESL educator also provides valuable expertise in other areas such as cross-cultural interviews and culturally responsive assessment devices and practices.

Speech/Language Specialist

Embedded within issues related to diversity is the need to ascertain differences between a language difference and a language disorder. One of the biggest misinterpretations made with ELLs is that their language needs are thought to be due to a disorder when in reality these needs frequently reflect typical and normal behaviors associated with stages of second language acquisition. Along with the bilingual/ESL educator, the speech/language specialists should provide expertise to the team in clarifying whether a language need is due to an intrinsic disorder or to naturally occurring stages in the acquisition of English as a second language.

Behavioral Specialist

This team member, who may include the school interventionist and/or social worker, should be included if the struggling learner exhibits social-emotional problems along with or separate from academic needs. A behavioral specialist provides much needed input related to completing and interpreting functional behavioral assessments as well as evidence-based interventions that should be included in behavioral support plans. The potential interrelationship between academic and social-emotional needs must be addressed by multi-tiered problem-solving teams to make the most accurate decisions concerning level or tier of intervention required.

Paraprofessional

In some educational situations, paraprofessionals are utilized to provide assistance to struggling learners. Their input and insights related to the students they assist should be included in the decisions made by problem-solving teams.

Parents/Guardians

The student's parents/guardians must be kept informed of progress throughout the multi-tiered instructional process. Input from the student's parents or guardians should be solicited to assist multi-tiered teams to understand ecological factors that may relate to the suspected need area. This is especially necessary if the struggling student is an English language learner, to avoid misinterpreting learning differences as disabilities due to lack of understanding of the effects of cultural/linguistic diversity on academic progress.

To further clarify the roles of team members, Form 7.1, adapted from Hoover (2009), provides a checklist to confirm that needed assessment team members make valued contributions based on areas of expertise. This guide should be used by standard treatment problem-solving teams to self-evaluate contributions of team members. While these are not all-inclusive, they represent some of the many areas of expertise that struggling learners are afforded as educators collaborate to make important multi-tiered RTI assessment decisions. For example, other members such as administrators, vision specialists, occupational therapists, or physical therapists need to be included as necessary.

In addition, within a standard treatment problem-solving model, several strengths emerge to allow the above team members to make the most informed decisions possible. These are summarized in Table 7.2, developed from information found in Brown-Chidsey and Steege (2005); Hoover (2009); and Ortiz, Wilkinson, Robertson-Courtney, & Kushner (2006).

Table 7.2   Strengths in the Standard Treatment Problem-Solving Model

Standard Treatment Problem-Solving Method

- utilizes rigorous, progress-monitoring data
- considers ecological factors relative to the suspected area of need
- includes input from a variety of sources and educational personnel in the decision-making process
- emphasizes the direct connection between classroom instruction and assessment results through implementation of different assessment practices (e.g., CBM, observations, work samples, review of records)
- facilitates positive support provided to general class teachers throughout the team decision-making process
- allows team members to consider a variety of evidence-based interventions to meet specific needs as instruction is adjusted

STANDARD TREATMENT PROBLEM-SOLVING TEAM PROCESS

Problem-solving models have been used in our nation's schools for several decades and provide a solid foundation to build upon as universal screening, progress monitoring, and diagnostic assessment results are used to make multi-tiered response to intervention decisions. Most models contain a series of steps that begin with initial identification of need followed by development and implementation of a plan to meet the need, concluding with some aspect of follow-up monitoring and continued decision making about student progress. One model frequently discussed includes steps and procedures identified from Deno (2005). Table 7.3 builds upon model discussions found in Brown-Chidsey and Steele (2005) and Deno (2005) as related to RTI assessment.

Table 7.3   Standard Treatment Problem-Solving Team Decision-Making Process

Step	*Key Components in Process*
1. Problem Identification	Universal screening in Tier 1 indicates a potential struggling learner; rate of progress is determined to be insufficient; magnitude of gap between actual and expected levels of performance is determined.
2. Problem Definition	Specific area of need is further clarified and delineated; academic and/or social-emotional skills requiring Tier 2 support are identified (e.g., reading fluency, behavior management, math computation).
3. Design Intervention Plan	Specific evidence-based intervention(s) to provide additional support in the academic or social-emotional areas pinpointed in Step 2 are selected; plan and time frame to implement intervention(s) are documented (e.g., thirty minutes/day–three days/week for five weeks); progress-monitoring devices and practices to be used to monitor effects of supplemental support are selected (e.g., CBM, classroom observation, task analysis, performance-based assessment); progress-monitoring timeline is documented (e.g., monitor progress weekly for five weeks).
4. Implement Intervention(s)	Evidence-based interventions are implemented with fidelity to provide Tier 2 supplemental support as documented in the intervention plan (Step 3); progress monitoring is implemented as designed; monitoring results are charted to illustrate trend of scores; gap analysis and rate of progress are determined.
5. Evaluate Progress	Progress-monitoring scores are interpreted to determine student's rate of progress and level of achievement toward achieving benchmarks or objective(s) emphasized in Tier 2 support; results from additional assessment practices employed (e.g., functional behavioral analysis, running records) are evaluated along with the charted progress-monitoring data.
6. Review/Refine Level of Intervention	Based on evaluated student progress (Step 5), decisions are made concerning whether: (a) another round of Tier 2 support is indicated, (b) Tier 2 support was successful and no longer necessary and discontinued, or (c) rate of progress and level of achievement indicate significant need and Tier 3 intervention is warranted (may include referral for diagnostic assessment for eligibility in special education).

Adhering to these six steps will assist multi-tiered problem-solving teams to make informed, comprehensive, relevant, and accurate decisions concerning the level of intensity, duration of implementation, and effective uses of standard treatment and related results to best educate struggling learners. Form 7.2 (Checklist for Implementing Standard Treatment Problem-Solving Model) provides a guide for teams to use to ensure that the six steps are adequately implemented. The guide reflects information discussed above to assist in clarifying effective implementation of a combined model to meet multi-tiered needs of struggling learners.

SUMMARY

Once assessment scores have been gathered and the process for obtaining the results has been implemented with fidelity, the task of accurately interpreting and applying the results becomes important for multi-tiered RTI problem-solving teams. This chapter discussed the recommended blended strengths from both the problem-solving and standard treatment protocol models for assessment decision making. Within this combined model, the roles of various assessment team members was discussed along with suggested steps to follow to effectively implement an assessment-team model to make the most informed decisions possible, based on the acquired screening, progress monitoring, or diagnostic assessment results.

Applying Chapter 7 Learning Outcomes

1. Describe the assessment-team process currently used in your school and evaluate it based on the process discussed in the chapter.

2. Identify the members of your assessment team and summarize their roles and involvement.

3. Design a plan to improve your existing assessment team's process so assessment results are more clearly understood and used in the multi-tiered instructional decision-making process.

4. Lead an assessment team meeting making certain that fidelity of assessment is discussed and corroborated for all assessment results considered.

Form 7.1   Checklist for Multi-Tier Assessment Team Members' Contributions

Student: _____ Date: _____

Instructions: Check each contribution made by the multi-tiered assessment team members.
Other contributions may be added as necessary.

General Class Teacher's Assessment Contributions

_____ Provide documented evidence of student's rate of progress toward achieving benchmarks.

_____ Present documentation of results of progress monitoring used in the classroom.

_____ Provide work samples relative to student's suspected learning or behavior problems.

_____ Share expertise of the content and process found within Tier 1 curriculum and instruction.

_____ Share charted progress-monitoring results over time.

_____ Confirm fidelity of implementation of classroom instruction and assessment.

_____ Assist with gap analysis and rate of progress procedures.

_____ Other:

Special Educator's Assessment Contributions

_____ Provide expertise in academic and social-emotional assessment of students with learning or behavior disorders.

_____ Interpret progress-monitoring results relative to suspected learning or behavior problems.

_____ Clarify opportunities to learn to meet suspected disability needs, including necessary differentiations or accommodations.

_____ Provide documentation to clarify extent to which an intrinsic disorder may be evident as established by the school/district RTI criteria.

_____ Collaborate with general educators in each tier of instruction.

_____ Ensure necessary assessment accommodations are implemented in each tier of instruction.

_____ Ensure the proper implementation of prereferral and referral procedures should learner be referred for special education.

_____ Assist with gap analysis and rate of progress procedures.

_____ Other:

Assessment Specialist's Contributions

_____ Present and/or clarify assessment scores.

_____ Present and discuss the evidence necessary to justify the selection and use of a particular device with the learner(s) in question.

_____ Assist classroom teachers with assessment fidelity issues and practices.

_____ Assist in conducting assessments as necessary.

_____ Provide valid assessment interpretations of assessment results.

(Continued)

Form 7.1 (Continued)

_____ Assist with gap analysis procedures to determine gap between expected and actual levels of performance.

_____ Ensure all team members understand the standard to which learner progress is compared (i.e., research norms; local norms; criterion based).

_____ Assist to clarify student rate of progress based on assessment scores/results.

_____ Other:

Content Area Specialist's (e.g., Interventionist) Assessment Contributions (Specify Content Area: _____)

_____ Provide knowledge/expertise in content field.

_____ Clarify learner's content area strengths/weaknesses.

_____ Assist in developing content area goals and objectives.

_____ Identify evidence-based interventions appropriate for the content area.

_____ Assist with ongoing progress-monitoring in content area.

_____ Assist with the selection of appropriate content area curriculum differentiations for each tier of instruction.

_____ Interpret content area screening, monitoring, or diagnostic assessment results.

_____ Assist with gap analysis and rate of progress procedures.

_____ Other:

ESL/Bilingual Educator's Assessment Contributions

_____ Discuss cultural or linguistic issues relative to suspected problem area.

_____ Ensure that response to intervention assessment is culturally responsive.

_____ Clarify student acculturation needs relative to suspected need area.

_____ Clarify behaviors expected in the acquisition of a second language.

_____ Implement cross-cultural assessment interviews.

_____ Assist in the valid interpretation and uses of assessment scores for diverse learners.

_____ Assist team to best discern learning differences from learning disabilities.

_____ Suggest culturally responsive assessment accommodations.

_____ Assist to clarify rate of progress and gap analysis results relative to cultural and linguistic needs.

_____ Other:

Speech/Language Specialist's Assessment Contributions

_____ Clarify assessment results related to language needs.

_____ Assist team to best discern language differences from language disorders.

_____ Provide speech/language progress-monitoring support.

_____ Provide suggestions for use of evidence-based speech/language interventions.

_____ Assist in accurately interpreting and using speech/language assessment scores to create valid instructional plans.

_____ Other:

Behavioral Specialist's (e.g., Interventionist) Assessment Contributions

_____ Provide expertise in the assessment of social-emotional needs.

_____ Assist in the implementation of functional behavioral assessment.

_____ Assist to ensure that behavioral assessments are completed with fidelity.

_____ Provide expertise on the relationships between observed behaviors and academic needs.

_____ Lead the development of valid behavioral intervention plans.

_____ Provide support for progress monitoring of social-emotional development in each tier.

_____ Assist with gap analysis and rate of progress procedures.

_____ Other:

Parents/Guardian's Assessment Contributions

_____ Provide perspective on suspected need from a view outside of the school.

_____ Discuss student's experiential background and prior educational experiences.

_____ Describe student's behaviors in community settings.

_____ Discuss student's academic abilities exhibited in the home.

_____ Discuss the use of both the native and English languages spoken in the home.

_____ Provide input into concerns and desires held for their child.

_____ Provide an overall perspective on how the learner socially interacts with others outside the school setting.

_____ Other:

Paraprofessional's Assessment Contributions

_____ Discuss tasks and completed work of the learner relative to suspected area of need.

_____ Assist in monitoring student progress toward academic and behavior goals/objectives.

_____ Provide input about student needs based on work completed with the student.

_____ Present student work samples.

_____ Assist with the charting of progress-monitoring data.

_____ Other:

Form 7.2 Checklist for Implementing Combined Standard Treatment Problem-Solving Model

Student: _____ Date: _____

Team Members: _____

Instructions: Check each item to evaluate proper implementation of your multi-tiered decision-making model for a student struggling in learning.

1. Problem Identification

____ Universal screening is completed.

____ Identification of potential struggling students is made.

____ Learner's rate of progress is identified.

____ Gap analysis procedures are completed.

____ Follow-up progress monitoring is conducted for suspected at-risk learners.

____ Screening and initial progress-monitoring data are charted to illustrate suspected learning or behavior need.

2. Problem Definition

____ Implementation of Tier 1 instruction with fidelity is confirmed.

____ Fidelity of assessment implementation is confirmed.

____ Validity of interpretation of assessment results is confirmed.

____ Rate of progress is confirmed.

____ Gap analysis results are confirmed.

____ Curricular differentiations previously completed are documented and discussed.

____ Each team member provides expertise to problem-solving process.

____ Specific area of need is clarified and pinpointed (e.g., reading fluency).

____ Standard treatment data and related authentic assessment results are used.

____ Influence of cultural and linguistic diversity needs are considered relative to suspected problem.

3. Intervention Plan Design

____ Need area is defined in terms of progress toward proficiency of benchmark or objective.

____ Expected rate of progress is determined.

____ Gap reduction targets are determined along with reasonable timeline.

____ Appropriate evidence-based assessments are selected.

____ A sufficient number of assessment devices/practices are selected to best monitor progress and explain assessment results (e.g., CBM, work sample analysis, performance-based).

____ Level and duration of support are determined (i.e., Tier 1, 2, 3 level of support).

____ Time frame for implementing support is established (e.g., three days/week for five weeks).

____ Process for monitoring student response to interventions is detailed (e.g., CBM).

____ Roles different educators will assume in implementing supports are clarified.

____ Supports to be provided to general educator are detailed.

___ Process for charting progress-monitoring data is clarified (e.g., computerized, teacher generated, commercial).

___ Implementation requirements necessary to successfully complete progress monitoring are discussed.

___ Procedures for documenting fidelity of assessment implementation are outlined.

___ Date(s) for future discussions to review instructional effects on student progress is established.

___ Established program is culturally responsive for diverse learners.

4. Intervention Plan Implementation

___ Evidence-based interventions are implemented with fidelity.

___ Progress monitoring is completed as designed and with fidelity.

___ Progress-monitoring results are charted over time.

___ Assessments completed relate directly to that which has been taught.

___ Implementation plan is completed the way in which it was designed.

___ Fidelity of assessment is corroborated based on procedures defined in implementation plan.

___ Implemented plan is culturally responsive for diverse learners.

5. Progress Evaluation

___ Team meets to review progress as outlined in implementation plan.

___ Rate of progress is considered along with level of proficiency.

___ Gap analysis is completed and updated based on progress.

___ Classroom-based assessment evidence is carefully considered relative to student rate of progress.

___ All team members apply their expertise to best clarify and interpret assessment results.

___ Effects of instruction are summarized.

___ Standard treatment data are considered along with related authentic classroom results.

___ Cultural responsive implementation is confirmed for diverse learners.

6. Intervention Plan Review/Revision

___ Intervention plan is revised based on progress-monitoring results.

___ Additional supports are provided if necessary.

___ Duration of interventions is extended if necessary.

___ Differentiations are identified as needed.

___ Decision concerning whether student remains with current level of support (i.e., Tier 2; 3) is made.

___ Revised implementation plan is generated.

___ Process for implementing revised plan is outlined including roles and supports to be provided to general educators.

___ Revised plan is implemented and dates to review student progress are determined.

8

Distinguishing Learning Differences From Disabilities Through RTI Assessment

SIGNIFICANCE TO CONTEMPORARY ASSESSMENT

Many struggling students in today's classrooms bring diverse cultural and linguistic backgrounds to the learning situation. For some, formal experiences with schooling may be very limited, while for others, prior experiences are quite different than what has been typically expected of learners across the grades. In addition, cultural values and norms for some learners may be significantly different than that which is usually seen in our classrooms. Also, the fact that many diverse learners are not fluent in English creates issues pertaining to the validity and reliability of assessment devices, practices, and—ultimately—the interpretations and uses of assessment scores. These issues are significant in today's schools since multi-tiered response to intervention assessment must assist educators to distinguish between a learning difference and a disability. Implementing culturally/linguistically appropriate RTI assessment practices and devices leads to valid assessment for diverse learners, including valid interpretation of scores and results.

CHAPTER OVERVIEW

Chapter 8 includes discussion of the unique issues associated with the implementation of RTI assessment for culturally and linguistically diverse learners. The topics of assessment bias and the implementation of culturally responsive assessment are addressed. In addition, several current educational practices that contribute to invalid assessment for diverse learners are discussed along with suggestions for preferred practices to reduce or minimize the effects of questionable assessment for these students. Suggestions and strategies to reduce misinterpreting learning differences as suspected disabilities are also provided.

Key Topics Addressed in Chapter

- ✦ Culturally Competent Assessment
- ✦ Difference Versus Disability
- ✦ Assessment Bias
- ✦ Cultural and Linguistic Ecological Factors

LEARNER OUTCOMES

Upon completion of Chapter 8, readers will

- acquire skills to implement culturally responsive RTI assessment
- be able to differentiate cultural and linguistic behaviors from disabilities
- evaluate the RTI assessment process for bias
- acquire skills to reduce bias decisions for diverse learners, including English language learners (ELLs)
- implement preferred educational practices to reduce the perpetuation of problematic practices often used with diverse learners

PERSONAL PERSPECTIVE

My educational experiences have afforded me the opportunity to work with diverse learners, their teachers, and families in high poverty areas in urban and rural locations in several states. As I shared in the Personal Perspective section in Chapter 3, these experiences along with my academic training provided me with extensive opportunities to see firsthand the interrelatedness of school, home, and community. My experiences in multicultural environments have benefited me in several ways relative to assessment. These include: (1) awareness that some behaviors of diverse learners are reflective of their cultural values and norms, (2) knowledge that a general understanding of a student's culture assists

(Continued)

(Continued)

a teacher to make education more relevant by valuing cultural experiences and preferences of the student, (3) ability to reduce misinterpreting learning differences as disabilities, and (4) understanding why many diverse learners are misplaced in special education and how to assist in reducing these misplacements.

Distinguishing learning differences from learning and behavior disorders is very challenging; however, adhering to the safeguards and best practices discussed in this chapter will help to best meet diverse learners' needs. I have seen many instances where the problematic prevailing practices discussed in this chapter have existed. For example, during my work in the southwest I developed a K–12 program for students with emotional/behavioral disorders, which included a school system on an Indian reservation. The majority of referrals that I received were for withdrawn, shy behavior. My knowledge of this particular culture assisted me to understand that these behaviors were showing signs of respect to adults reflecting a cultural value. Teachers who did not understand this cultural value misinterpreted the behaviors as signs of a potential emotional/behavioral disorder.

While many other examples could be shared, I believe that the ultimate message is that when we are working and teaching within diverse cultures and with students from culturally and linguistically diverse backgrounds, it is essential to, at a minimum, acquire a general knowledge about the culture. This knowledge assisted me to avoid misinterpreting the behaviors discussed in this chapter as disorders, thereby reducing overrepresentation of diverse learners in special education. I believe that an understanding of the topics discussed in this chapter will assist educators to make more informed and accurate instructional progress-monitoring decisions for diverse learners educated within RTI multi-tiered instructional models. This, in turn, leads to a reduction in the number of unnecessary referrals and placement into special education of diverse students.

MISINTERPRETING LEARNING DIFFERENCE AS LEARNING DISABILITY

In order for multi-tiered response to intervention to be effective, it must meet the needs of all culturally and linguistically diverse learners, including those who are in the process of learning English as a second language. Although a variety of factors account for the educational difficulties experienced by diverse learners, three of the more significant issues that relate directly to effective RTI assessment are:

- identification of current educational practices that perpetuate misinterpreting differences as disabilities
- implementation of culturally proficient education
- strategies for distinguishing learning differences from disabilities

An understanding of each of these issues provides multi-tiered problem-solving teams with knowledge and expertise necessary to implement appropriate tiered interventions to diverse learners.

Prevailing Educational Practices

The misidentification of diverse learners as having a disability rather than learning differences can be traced to several current practices regularly seen in today's schools and classrooms. Discussed below are several of these practices, developed from my experiences as well as a variety of sources (Baca & Cervantes, 2004; Hoover, 2009; Hoover, Klingner, Baca, & Patton, 2008; Klingner, Sorrells, & Barrera, 2007), along with suggestions for executing necessary change to 'preferred practices' to best meet diverse learners' needs within multi-tiered RTI assessment. These are not presented in any order of importance as each represents a significant concern in the education of diverse learners.

Note: Each of the "Prevailing Practices" presented here reflect existing occurrences that need to be eliminated to best meet assessment needs of diverse learners. Drawing attention to that which we should be avoiding is sometimes necessary, especially if the practice has been implemented for many years. Therefore, while the prevailing practices are presented as tasks we need to avoid, "Preferred Practices" are also provided to help move toward a more desirable assessment process for diverse learners.

Prevailing Practice 1: Lack of Multicultural Perspectives

> **RTI Assessment Question:** Do all educators involved with the education of diverse learners struggling in school possess culturally competent teaching preparation and teaching abilities?

Description: Many teacher education programs for general and special educators provide minimal emphasis on the education of diverse learners, resulting in a teaching force lacking in-depth perspectives on educational issues and best practices for culturally and linguistically diverse learners.

Preferred Practice: All educators should be provided training and experiences in the teaching and learning of diverse students to best incorporate cultural values, norms, and expectations into everyday instruction. In addition, a working knowledge of the process required to learn a second language should be understood by all along with best practices.

Suggestions to Achieve Preferred Practice: Educators who are currently enrolled in a teacher preparation program should take a minimum of three courses addressing the topic of teaching culturally and linguistically diverse learners, including those with disabilities. For those who already hold a teacher degree, a comprehensive professional development program can be developed and implemented by completing courses, workshops, conference sessions, etc. on the topic of meeting the needs of diverse learners in today's schools, including those directly addressing multi-tiered RTI for diverse learners.

Significance to Multi-Tiered RTI Assessment: The successful assessment and progress monitoring of diverse learners must accommodate and account for unique learning needs and preferences due to cultural and linguistic differences. As will be discussed in the remaining Prevailing Practices sections, assessment for diverse learners cannot be valid or reliable if learning differences are not considered and incorporated into the decision making by problem-solving teams. This includes classroom instruction implemented by educators who understand and value diverse cultural customs, languages, preferred styles of learning, and related home and community ecological variables such as those addressed in Chapter 3. Professional development and/or teacher preparation programs need to provide additional emphasis on the education of this ever-growing population of students in today's schools, to best implement multi-tiered assessment procedures and practices for all learners.

Prevailing Practice 2: Failure to Accommodate Diverse Cultural Values and Norms Into Everyday Curriculum Implementation

> **RTI Assessment Question:** In what ways are learners' cultural values and norms reflected within the context of daily instruction and assessment?

Description: Diverse learner's family and community values, customs, and needs reflective of cultural and linguistic diversity are generally not incorporated into everyday curriculum, facilitating a situation where curricular topics, interventions, and assessments lack relevance for many diverse students.

Preferred Practice: Incorporation of diverse customs and values should be implemented in daily curriculum to best provide diverse learners with a relevant context from which they may more actively participate in class activities, discussions, and associated assessments.

Suggestions to Achieve Preferred Practice: Many opportunities exist to make daily instruction contextually relevant to diverse learners such as: (1) drawing analogies to similar situations or topics across cultures; (2) facilitating student sharing of own diverse experiences reflecting their different cultures, values, or preferred practices; or (3) incorporating opportunities for all learners to explore different values, customs, and contributions into required assignments.

Significance to Multi-Tiered RTI Assessment: Relevance in learning is as basic a premise for success with students as any we see in education. This is an issue for all learners and within all educational contexts. Concerning multi-tiered RTI assessment, valid and reliable results can only occur if the assessment devices, practices, and uses of assessment scores are relevant to the particular population. Multi-tiered progress monitoring will only be effective for diverse learners if it contains the fundamental elements previously discussed throughout this book. Failure to accommodate for diversity in RTI assessment may lead problem-solving teams down a path of making uninformed and erroneous decisions concerning progress toward benchmarks or objectives.

Prevailing Practice 3: Misinterpretation of Language Differences as Language or Reading Disabilities

> **RTI Assessment Question:** What safeguards are in place to ensure that limited English proficiency is viewed as a language difference and not a language disorder?

Description: Misinterpretation occurs when diverse learners' assessment results and classroom performances are viewed as language or reading disabilities, when in many instances they are learning differences reflective of cultural and linguistic diversity.

Preferred Practice: Consideration of the stage of second language acquisition within which a learner operates should be made prior to interpreting assessment scores and classroom performances as reflecting "intrinsic" problems.

Suggestions to Achieve Preferred Practice: Anyone directly involved in the education of a student in the process of acquiring English as a second language must, at a minimum, be familiar with the stages of second language acquisition and its impact on classroom performance or testing situations, especially as related to language and reading development. Behaviors that appear to be a disorder may in fact be typical and normal for the learner in his/her development of a second language.

Significance to Multi-Tiered RTI Assessment: Understanding behaviors associated with second language acquisition (See Table 8.4) is critical to making informed multi-tiered RTI decisions for diverse learners, especially as it relates to "rate of progress" related to reading development. A learner's rate of progress may be slower than others but commensurate with the language acquisition stage the learner is operating within at the time of the progress monitoring. Familiarity with behaviors typical of second language acquisition will help to ensure that multi-tier problem-solving teams are making informed and valid decisions for diverse learners in today's schools. As a result, becoming knowledgeable of second language development reduces misinterpretations about reading or language disabilities. The reader is referred to Baca and Cervantes (2004) for a more detailed discussion of second language acquisition.

Prevailing Practice 4: Lack of Knowledge and Understanding of the Effects of Acculturation on Student Progress in Learning

> **RTI Assessment Question:** How are the effects of adapting to a new environment such as a new community, school, and classroom considered in assessment decision making for diverse learners?

Description: Many educators lack an understanding of what it entails to adapt (i.e., acculturate) to new environments, which may include students exhibiting various behaviors often misunderstood as behavior disorders. Many culturally and linguistically diverse learners must acculturate to new community, school, or classroom environments; adjustments to these new environments affect students in different ways.

Preferred Practice: Educators must understand behaviors typically associated with acculturation. These include behaviors such as extreme stress, withdrawal, unresponsiveness, or confusion with locus of control. For most students, these behaviors are temporary and will subside as the student becomes more acculturated to new community, school, or classroom environments.

Suggestions to Achieve Preferred Practice: As previously discussed, educators who engage in professional development to better understand culturally and linguistically diverse learners should include knowledge about acculturation. In addition, the application of this knowledge in understanding academic and social-emotional progress and development is essential to best provide effective education to diverse learners. Educators should complete workshops or courses that discuss acculturation to prepare themselves to make informed decisions about diverse learners.

Significance to Multi-Tiered RTI Assessment: Failure to consider acculturation effects may lead to at least three problematic situations in multi-tiered RTI: (1) perception that "rate of progress" is insufficient when in reality it may be typical for the level of acculturation the learner is experiencing, (2) decision to provide the learner with more intensive intervention than necessary due to lack of understanding of acculturative effects, or (3) misinterpreted behaviors that lead to an erroneous referral for a full special education evaluation. Familiarity with acculturation and its effects on student learning and response to instruction leads to selection and use of the most appropriate evidence-based assessment practices to monitor progress of diverse learners.

Prevailing Practice 5: Mismatch between Teaching and Student Instructional Preferences

RTI Assessment Question: In what ways are teacher preferences compatible with a struggling student's preferences toward learning?

Description: Cultural and linguistic values, customs, and norms shape a learner's preferences toward various types of interventions (e.g., cooperative versus competitive, group versus independent, holistic versus discrete). Oftentimes, these student preferences are not compatible with the teacher's preferred teaching styles, creating the perception that something is intrinsically wrong with the learner—rather than a difference between preferred styles of learning and teaching.

Preferred Practice: The preferred situation is that all educators value diversity and make every effort possible to be certain that the manner and conditions in which a student is assessed reflect compatibility between preferred teacher and student styles, so a mismatch is avoided.

Suggestions to Achieve Preferred Practice: To avoid a teaching and learning style mismatch, educators should choose evidence-based interventions that do not conflict with diverse students' values and norms, while simultaneously creating a flexible classroom environment that promotes acceptance of diversity on a daily basis. For example, some students prefer a longer wait time prior to responding to a question, desire to share information rather than keep things to themselves, or choose to listen as a primary means of learning. In most situations, these behaviors are not indications of a disorder; rather, they are differences that should be accommodated to ensure accurate instruction and assessment results.

Significance to Multi-Tiered RTI Assessment: Monitoring effects of that which is taught to a student in the classroom must include consideration of various factors that may assist to explain results for diverse learners. Multi-tiered problem-solving teams must make certain that perceived lack of progress or slower rate of progress is not due to incompatible teaching and learning styles. If a mismatch is identified, other evidence-based interventions should be attempted with continued monitoring of progress. In many situations, simply changing an intervention to one that reflects compatibility between teaching and learning preferences will lead to more accurate assessment evidence concerning adequate rate of progress towards mastery of targeted benchmarks or objectives.

Prevailing Practice 6: Lack of Culturally Proficient Assessment

RTI Assessment Question: In what ways are the assessment practices and selected instruments appropriate for use with struggling learners from culturally and linguistically diverse backgrounds?

Description: Educators who lack cultural proficiency in teaching and learning often unknowingly implement inappropriate assessment to diverse learners by not considering their cultural and linguistic values.

Preferred Practice: The preferred practice is that all diverse learners are assessed by educators who are, at minimum, culturally competent. In addition, educators in today's classrooms should determine their own level of cultural competence or proficiency, evaluate the extent to which cultural diversity is accommodated within their classroom-based assessments, and demonstrate that the manner in which they implement evidence-based assessment reflects cultural proficiency.

Suggestions to Achieve Preferred Practice: Educators become culturally competent or proficient in assessment by: (1) learning about different cultures; (2) understanding their own heritage, background, and views toward diversity; (3) engaging in dialogue and professional development on cultural diversity; and (4) applying developed competence in progress monitoring and related assessment practices. The process for achieving cultural competence and proficiency in education is a six-stage process that is discussed in greater detail in a subsequent section in this chapter. However, as will be discussed, educators at the cultural competent or cultural proficient stage are best prepared to implement culturally responsive assessment.

Significance to Multi-Tiered RTI Assessment. Cultural proficiency in education provides the foundation for ensuring that all diverse learners are provided appropriate assessment and progress monitoring. Multi-tiered problem-solving teams should ensure that cultural competent assessment is conducted to make the most informed decisions about the most appropriate level or tier of intervention for diverse learners. Failure to implement culturally responsive assessment in multi-tiered instruction contributes to erroneous interpretations of screening, progress monitoring, or diagnostic data for diverse learners.

Prevailing Practice 7: Failure to Consider Both First and Second Languages

RTI Assessment Question: If a disability is suspected, do similar characteristics and behaviors exist when the bilingual students use both native and English languages?

Description: In many assessment situations, diverse learners more fluent in their first language (e.g., Spanish, Hmong) are tested in their less proficient second language (i.e., English). This leads directly to invalid results and associated erroneous decisions concerning suspected disabilities.

Preferred Practice: The preferred practice is that all learners are assessed using their most proficient language and/or English if bilingual. This may include use of assessment devices in the native language; if not possible, assessment should be made through use of properly trained translators/interpreters.

Suggestions to Achieve Preferred Practice: One of the initial tasks educators must complete to best understand the role of language in assessment is to acquire a working knowledge and understanding of validity and reliability of assessment devices, practices, and uses of results. An understanding of these important elements provides a solid foundation to the proper selection, administration, scoring, and interpretation of assessment results for diverse learners. Once this knowledge is developed, educators must apply that knowledge and avoid use of assessment devices and practices that do not accommodate language needs of English language learners (ELLs).

Significance to Multi-Tiered RTI Assessment: Prior to any RTI assessment, the language proficiency levels of diverse learners must be identified. Multi-tiered problem-solving teams must advocate for diverse learners by ensuring that all assessment and progress monitoring is completed in the student's most proficient language. In addition, if English is not the student's most proficient language, then assessment should be conducted in both languages prior to identifying a disability. It is also essential that problem-solving teams bear in mind that perceived language problems may in fact reflect typical and normal behaviors for the student, based on the learner's stage of second language development and/or effects of acculturation and not a disability.

Prevailing Practice 8: Insufficient Learning and Assessment Opportunities

RTI Assessment Question: What documentation exists to confirm that the diverse learner who is struggling has been provided sufficient opportunities to adequately demonstrate progress?

Description: Many culturally and linguistically diverse learners are provided insufficient time or opportunity to master skills or complete assessments. Too often, educators provide students with tasks or activities that lack cultural relevance or fail to provide additional time for task completion. This, in turn, leads to decisions that suggest a student has a learning problem when in reality all that is required are additional opportunities within the instructional and assessment process.

Preferred Practice: Assessment for diverse learners should include documentation and evidence that the learner was provided adequate time and relevant evidence-based instruction. Should it be determined that the learner requires more time and opportunity in Tier 1 or 2 instruction, this should be provided to avoid misinterpreting lack of progress as lack of opportunity.

Suggestions to Achieve Preferred Practice: Multi-tiered problem-solving teams should use a guide or checklist to document sufficient opportunities to learn. Sufficient opportunities include classroom factors such as using appropriate and relevant materials, evidence-based interventions, and classroom management procedures that reflect the cultural and linguistic diversity students bring to the learning environment. In addition, students must be provided sufficient opportunities to become knowledgeable of the progress monitoring and other assessment practices or devices. Lack of familiarity with assessment procedures, devices, or practices can yield inaccurate assessment results; this, in turn, leads to misinterpretation of scores as indicators of disabilities.

Significance to Multi-Tiered RTI Assessment: Sufficient opportunities to learn in both classroom and assessment situations are critical to obtaining valid and reliable assessment scores. This is then necessary for making valid decisions concerning uses of those obtained assessment scores. Multi-tiered RTI problem-solving teams have a genuine responsibility to ensure that all diverse learners are provided quality, research-based universal screening in Tier 1 and, if necessary, appropriate progress monitoring in Tier 2. The extent to which either of these assessments is reflective of insufficient opportunities to learn—in the classroom or in understanding the assessment itself—relates directly to inaccurate decisions and the possibility of erroneously denying needed services or initiating services not appropriate to the student. Decisions concerning lack of progress in any tier of instruction must initially include determination that the diverse student has had sufficient and culturally responsive opportunities to learn both in instruction and in understanding required assessment.

Prevailing Practice 9: Use of Biased Assessment Practices and Devices

> **RTI Assessment Question:** What assurances exist that confirm unbiased assessment practices and instruments are used with diverse learners who struggle in school?

Description: Bias continues to exist in many aspects of assessment for culturally and linguistically diverse learners in today's classrooms and schools. This results directly from the continued use of inappropriate instruments and practices with diverse learners, whether classroom-based or districtwide assessments, as well as problematic decisions generated from the assessment scores.

Preferred Practice: The preferred practice is that all assessment for diverse learners adheres to unbiased practices, and that the interpretation and uses of assessment scores be completed by culturally responsive assessment personnel.

Suggestions to Achieve Preferred Practice: Similar to the discussion about language issues in assessment, reducing bias begins with understanding validity and reliability in assessment. Problem-solving team members who are knowledgeable about ways to discern possible bias provide valuable insights into decisions concerning level and intensity of instruction for diverse learners. Multi-tiered assessment teams should check for possible bias in instruments, practices, and uses of results to reduce biased assessment for diverse learners.

Significance to Multi-Tiered RTI Assessment: Unbiased assessment is central to providing appropriate multi-tiered instruction to diverse learners. Any multi-tiered problem-solving team must be certain that the assessment devices and practices are relevant and appropriate for use with diverse learners prior to their implementation. Simply using devices and practices because they are used with all other students is not an acceptable rationale for use with some diverse learners. Problem-solving teams have a professional responsibility to know the validity and reliability of any assessment device and practice used. This is initially determined through documentation provided by research and/or assessment device developers. Table 8.1, developed from discussions about reducing bias (Baca & Cervantes, 2004; Hoover, Klingner et al., 2008; Klingner, Hoover & Baca, 2008) provides examples of possible explanations to the behavior indicators that may be exhibited by diverse learners. Assessment teams that respect diverse cultural values or linguistic needs, such as those presented in the table are in the best position to minimize assessment bias.

Table 8.1   Behavioral Types That May Reflect Cultural/Linguistic Diversity in RTI Assessment

---

Type: Quiet/Withdrawn Behaviors

Behavior Indicators: Remains quiet in the classroom or exhibits extended periods of silence; shy and prefers to be alone; remains quiet around authority figures (e.g., teacher).

Minimizing Bias: Students acquiring a second language experience normal periods of extended silence. Some cultures teach children to remain quiet around authority figures as a sign of respect, and students not familiar with expectations in U.S. schools may initially appear uncertain and withdraw while they learn expectations.

Type: Aggressive/Acting Out Behaviors

Behavior Indicators: Exhibits assertive behaviors; stands up for self in a disagreement; exhibits acting out behaviors counter to classroom expectations.

Minimizing Bias: Some cultures teach students to not back down in times of disagreements with others. Lack of experience with expected U.S. classroom behavioral expectations may result in anxiety for some students leading to acting out behavior.

Type: Varied Perceptions Toward Daily Living Items/Tasks

Behavior Indicators: May possess perceptions about everyday items such as time, sharing of items, personal space, or gender roles that are different from what is typically seen in U.S. classrooms.

Minimizing Bias: Cultures vary in their views of time, often relying on task-driven expectations/completion rather than minutes on a clock. Sharing of belongings is highly valued in some cultures, which leads students to share with each other in the classroom (may be misinterpreted as cheating/stealing). Some cultures teach that certain tasks or subject areas are more male or female dominant, and therefore avoid based on gender.

Type: Confusion With Student and Teacher Class Expectations

Behavior Indicators: Prefers cooperative group work over independent or competitive tasks; preferred styles of learning may differ from preferred teaching practices.

Minimizing Bias: Some cultures teach students that working together is more productive and encouraged. Students acculturating or acquiring a second language may prefer to use different styles of learning, which may differ from the teaching styles used in the classroom.

PREVAILING PRACTICES: CONCLUDING THOUGHTS

Most educators in today's schools can identify with one or more of these problematic prevailing practices, and those of us who have been in the field for several years can reflect on situations where each of these occurred. Today, it is no longer "OK" to lack awareness of these debilitating prevailing practices. While not all-inclusive, these selected practices exist and will continue to exist if we do not confront them and strive to reduce their occurrence. As we move into the newest model for educating all students—including diverse learners— multi-tiered RTI problem-solving teams have a unique opportunity to ensure that these problematic assessment practices do not occur in schools or districts through thoughtful and informative uses of universal screening, progress monitoring, or diagnostic assessment. Form 8.1 provides a checklist for determining extent to which *preferred practices* exist in each school for ELLs. Adherence to these assists to reduce bias and in turn reduces misplacements of diverse learners into special education.

In regard to referrals for special education, the following tasks should be considered prior to referring a culturally and linguistically diverse learner to special education. This list below was developed from discussions about referral considerations for diverse learners (Baca & Cervantes, 2004; Hoover, Klingner et al., (2008); Klingner, Hoover, & Baca, 2008). A culturally responsive referral to special education reflects the following educational practices:

- use of most proficient instructional and assessment language
- use of authentic, classroom-based assessments
- compatibility between teaching styles and preferred student learning styles
- incorporation of results from classroom observations and interviews with parents and teachers in assessment decision making
- use of culturally responsive universal screening and progress-monitoring procedures and devices
- level or stage of acculturation is accommodated
- sufficient opportunities to learn provided and documented

These practices help guide problem-solving team decisions concerning the validity in uses of assessment scores and the appropriateness of referring a diverse learner for special education in an unbiased manner.

CULTURALLY RESPONSIVE ASSESSMENT

Culturally responsive assessment occurs when educators understand and apply cultural and linguistic values and norms into the assessment process for diverse learners. For most educators, this is a lifelong process that requires professional development to maintain positive attitudes and practices where diversity is genuinely incorporated into daily teaching. This process is typically viewed as a six-stage process as discussed by Gay (2000), Hoover, Klingner et al. (2008), and Mason (1993) as illustrated in Table 8.2.

Table 8.2   Stages to Achieving Culturally Responsive Education

Stage	Description	Significance to Multi-Tiered Assessment
Cultural Destructiveness	Cultural contributions are not acknowledged or viewed as problems; no evidence of cultural diversity is found in curriculum implementation.	Lack of acknowledgment of cultural contributions leads to selection of inappropriate devices/practices and to very narrow and biased interpretations of assessment scores.
Cultural Incapacity	Cultural identity is ignored or viewed indifferently in education, or identity is viewed as insignificant.	Cultural indifference in teaching also reflects indifference in assessment, which perpetuates many of the inappropriate "prevailing practices" leading to decisions that can significantly interfere with determining correct levels or tiers of interventions.
Cultural Blindness	Educators acknowledge that cultural diversity exists, yet cultural differences are viewed as unimportant with little significance to the implementation of curriculum.	Blindness toward importance of culture in curriculum is also reflected in blindness toward role of culture in universal screening and progress monitoring, which leads to skewed results and inappropriate selection of proper tier of intervention.
Cultural Precompetence	Cultural diversity is acknowledged and valued; educators engage in professional development to increase their cultural competence and make some efforts to incorporate cultural and linguistic values in curriculum implementation.	Precompetence is the first stage where issues of assessment can be culturally relevant in screening, monitoring, and diagnostic assessment; however, this can be surface level requiring further growth toward proficiency.
Cultural Competence	Culture is genuinely valued; cultural values are incorporated into classroom instruction; continued professional development exists to increase personal cultural responsiveness.	Effective assessment for diverse learners can be implemented on a regular basis once multi-tiered problem-solving team members and other educators achieve cultural competence.
Cultural Proficiency	Cultural values and diversity are significantly embedded into the development and implementation of curriculum; educators address culturally diverse ideals in all aspects of education.	Culturally proficient educators take culturally responsive assessment to the highest level and provide the necessary leadership on multi-tiered RTI problem-solving teams.

As shown, each stage gradually assists educators to progress toward a more culturally competent or proficient level. Also, as described, attributes (both positive and negative) for the different stages have a direct impact on multi-tiered response to intervention assessments. Educators, especially those on problem-solving teams, should evaluate their own cultural competence levels and create professional development plans to improve skills in this progression. This type of plan could be developed with a colleague to collaboratively pursue more competent or proficient assessment for diverse learners.

Cultural competence leads to selection and use of culturally responsive screening, monitoring, and diagnostic assessments. Chapter 5 described several assessment *practices* and each of these is appropriate for use with diverse learners. However, the selection and use of assessment *devices* present more challenges to educators as many of these instruments are inappropriately used with diverse learners due to lack of research with this specific population. Form 8.2 provides a checklist to apply to assessment devices to determine appropriateness for use with diverse learners. The checklist, developed from information found in Baca and Cervantes (2004), and Klingner, Hoover, and Baca (2008) guides educators in their decisions concerning the appropriateness of an assessment device for use with culturally and linguistically diverse learners. In addition, several specific culturally responsive practices have been identified in Table 8.3. This table, developed from discussions about unbiased assessment by the National Center for Culturally Responsive Teaching (NCCRESt) (2005) as well as in Hoover (2009), Klingner and Edwards (2006), and Wiley (1996), presents several best practices to assist in reducing assessment bias.

Table 8.3   Culturally Responsive Practices and RTI Assessment

Culturally Responsive Practices	*Significance to Multi-Tiered Assessment*
Connect with students by learning about their diverse environmental contexts.	Knowledge of diverse cultural environments assists educators to put assessment results in a relevant context for diverse learners.
Respect preferred communication and learning styles of students.	Necessary assessment accommodations may best be made if educators understand the cultural influences on communication and preferred learning styles of diverse learners.
Incorporate diverse community practices and values in the implementation of curriculum.	Knowledge of the ways in which diverse communities value education assists in the selection of relevant assessment practices.
Differentiate instruction to meet acculturation needs.	Knowledge of the factors associated with acculturation assist problem-solving teams to more accurately interpret behaviors observed during the assessment of diverse learners.
Develop students' linguistic competence through functional language use in classroom dialogue.	Assessment of students in the process of acquiring a second language should focus on authentic, functional language use.
Draw upon students' experiential background in classroom instruction.	Experiential background provides problem-solving teams valuable insights into learners' assessment results and rate of progress.

Culturally Responsive Practices	Significance to Multi-Tiered Assessment
Contextualize learning (i.e., draw from students' native values/norms).	Extent to which families and communities value assessment assists problem-solving teams to best interpret assessment scores and student approach to the assessment situation.
Provide cognitively challenging evidence-based interventions and curricula.	Assessment should include determining student use of higher order thinking abilities to obtain the most meaningful and accurate results for diverse learners.
Facilitate cooperative learning, including group work.	Knowledge that some diverse learners prefer and are more successful with cooperative learning education, including group learning, may assist to explain questionable competitive and individual assessment results.

Educators pursue a lifelong process in becoming culturally proficient, which typically includes completion of university coursework, practical experiences in the field, and professional development to build upon and upgrade knowledge and skills. However, as previously presented, one of the problematic "prevailing practices" is the lack of formal training and associated experiences in multicultural education, which may lead to an uninformed or misinformed segment of the education workforce. Therefore, it is imperative that multitiered RTI problem-solving teams ensure that members: (1) value diversity; (2) understand the role and influence that diverse needs may have on universal screening, progress monitoring, and diagnostic assessment results; (3) continue to further develop cultural proficiency; and (4) self-check the decisions made to ensure they are based on culturally responsive assessment.

Distinguishing Difference From Disability

Ensuring that the most appropriate and relevant assessment occurs for diverse learners assists to address one of the most fundamental issues challenging educators in multi-tiered response to intervention—that is, distinguishing cultural and linguistic diverse needs and behaviors from intrinsic disabilities. To assist in distinguishing these differences, Table 8.4 provides an overview of selected behaviors often associated with learning or behavior disorders and those reflective of cultural and linguistic differences.

As illustrated, various behaviors typically expected from students in different stages of second language acquisition are similar to those typically attributed to learning or behavior disorders. In addition, behaviors reflective of diverse cultural values may be misinterpreted as disorders due to the lack of understanding of cultural influences on student actions, perceptions, or attitudes. In short, behavioral differences due to cultural and linguistic diversity must not be misinterpreted by multi-tiered teams as learning or behavior disorders. Adherence to the various assessment practices previously discussed along with consideration of the behaviors presented in Table 8.4, assists educators to reduce the problems associated with misidentifying learning differences as disabilities.

Table 8.4 Differentiating Learning Differences From Learning/Behavior Problems

---

Types of Behaviors Often Associated With Learning or Behavior Disorders

- overactivity, distractibility, aggression, withdrawal, anxiety
- reading miscues, fluency deficits, comprehension needs
- math reasoning problems, calculation needs
- vocabulary deficits
- falling below expected classroom academic achievement levels based on grade/age
- insufficient rate of academic and/or behavioral progress
- inability to respond to quality instruction
- short/long term memory deficits

Difference Versus Disability Decision-Making Concerns: These and similar behaviors should not be misinterpreted as disorders if they reflect cultural/linguistic diversity.

Types of Behaviors Influenced by Cultural Diversity

- differences in how time is perceived
- varied preferences toward learning styles
- time needed to best deal with the process of adapting to new cultural environments
- oral versus written traditions in learning
- preference toward cooperative, paired, independent, or competitive learning
- strategies for managing time and organizing tasks

Difference Versus Disability Decision-Making Concerns: Various cultures may perceive these and similar behaviors in a variety of ways reflecting cultural values, and should not be misinterpreted as disorders because they are different than typical expectations in the classroom.

Types of Behaviors Associated With Process of Acquiring English as a Second Language

- extended periods of nonverbal or silent behaviors (i.e., active listening)
- difficulty in the use of English vocabulary during initial stages of development
- systematic development of English words over an extended period of time
- appearing inattentive while attempting to acquire a second language
- frustration/withdrawal reflecting challenges in acquiring a second language
- problems responding to others during early stages of acquiring English
- consistent progress in appropriate use of English if provided sufficient time
- frequent grammar errors evident especially during early stages of English development
- requires longer "wait time" before responding to question or statement

Difference Versus Disability Decision-Making Concerns: These and related behaviors are typical during the development of a second language and must be interpreted as expected, normal behaviors and not language or learning disorders.

Source: Hoover (2009). Reprinted by permission.

In addition, assessment for diverse learners must be conducted in the most proficient language and in both languages if neither language is fully developed. *Only by observing similar academic or social-emotional problematic behaviors in both languages and evident in both cultures can an intrinsic disorder be considered.* In many instances, students may experience problems when using English yet demonstrate average or above development in those same abilities when assessed in their native language. To this end, five essential principles that educators should adhere to in the implementation of curriculum and associated assessment can be identified to meet the needs of diverse learners struggling in school. These are presented below and reflect many of the assessment ideas presented throughout this book.

Assessment Principle 1. Multi-tiered response to intervention assessment should be reflective of student's culture, experiential background, primary language, and family and community values.

Assessment Principle 2. Multi-tiered response to intervention assessment should consider the integrated content knowledge and skills that students possess.

Assessment Principle 3. Multi-tiered response to intervention assessment must include consideration of both cognitive and academic skills in culturally responsive ways.

Assessment Principle 4. Multi-tiered response to intervention assessment should reflect high-level learning expectations and outcomes for all students.

Assessment Principle 5. Multi-tiered response to intervention assessment must include authentic and inquiry-based learning tasks.

Adherence to these basic assessment principles provides diverse learners the best opportunities to demonstrate their true knowledge, skills, and abilities in universal screening, progress monitoring, and diagnostic assessment. Multi-tiered RTI problem-solving teams should establish and maintain the highest standards for themselves in their development as culturally responsive educators. Distinguishing learning differences from learning or behavior disorders is central to effective multi-tiered response to intervention for all learners.

Chapter 8 concludes with a checklist containing a variety of items within ten key educational areas that educators should consider to ensure effective assessment for diverse learners within RTI models. Form 8.3, developed from information found in Baca and Cervantes (2004), Hoover, Klingner et al. (2008), Klingner, Hoover, and Baca (2008), should be completed by assessment teams to make certain that the many issues that must be addressed to implement culturally responsive assessment are incorporated into the decision-making process. These items reflect various assessment and instructional aspects that support implementation of preferred practices and will assist to avoid the problematic practices presented in this chapter. The extent to which the items on Form 8.3 are addressed and considered in the overall RTI assessment procedures will assist to ensure the most appropriate assessment for diverse learners.

SUMMARY

One of the most significant challenges found within multi-tiered response to intervention assessment is the need to replace the various problematic practices that have led to erroneous or otherwise invalid assessment scores and results for diverse learners. Nine of these questionable practices were presented along with suggestions for preferred practices for educators to implement in schools.

Ultimately, multi-tiered models must include more effective culturally responsive assessment than has been completed over the past several decades to best benefit all students, including culturally and linguistically diverse learners.

Central to more effective assessment for diverse learners is the multi-tiered assessment team's ability to discern learning differences from learning or behavior disabilities as discussed throughout this chapter.

Applying Chapter 8 Learning Outcomes

1. Evaluate your school's current assessment practices to determine the extent to which one or more of the questionable prevailing practices are implemented.

2. Prepare and deliver a PowerPoint presentation to your school's faculty that discusses how to determine learning differences from learning disabilities (Table 8.4).

3. Evaluate your current level of cultural competence and create a professional development plan to further develop skills and abilities in this area.

4. Lead a discussion with your assessment team on cultural proficiency and its relationship to making informed assessment decisions for culturally and linguistically diverse learners in your multi-tiered RTI model.

Form 8.1   Checklist for Evidence of Use of Preferred Assessment Practices With Struggling ELLs

Student: _____ Date: _____

Suspected Area of Need: _____

Instructions: Check each item and provide a descriptive statement demonstrating use of the item with diverse learners within multi-tiered response to intervention assessment relative to the need.

____ Learner is provided sufficient opportunities in the assessment process to demonstrate acquired knowledge and skills.

Descriptive Evidence:

____ Appropriate evidence-based assessment is implemented in culturally-responsive ways.

Descriptive Evidence:

____ Assessment reflects challenging tasks including emphasis on higher-level thinking.

Descriptive Evidence:

____ Assessment accounts for acculturation needs.

Descriptive Evidence:

____ Assessment is conducted in the most proficient language and/or English if bilingual.

Descriptive Evidence:

____ Assessment practices are compatible with preferred ways of learning consistent with cultural values/norms.

Descriptive Evidence:

____ Assessment is implemented by a culturally competent educator.
Descriptive Evidence:

____ Unbiased Assessment is completed with fidelity.

Descriptive Evidence:

Form 8.2   Checklist for Selecting Culturally Responsive Assessment Devices

Student: _____

Assessment Device: _____

Circle Yes (Y) or No (N) for each item as it applies to the assessment device. Record descriptive comments to provide further documentation of cultural responsiveness of the device. Attach completed guide to assessment device protocol.

Device avoids use of culturally insensitive or inappropriate items.   **Y**   **N**
Comments:

A sufficient representative sample of diverse learners was included in the
norming and standardization of the instrument.   **Y**   **N**
Comments:

Instrument's manual clearly describes the necessary steps to administer the   **Y**   **N**
device in a manner consistent with its development.
Comments:

Instruments translated into a different language (e.g., Spanish) were developed
using proper translation procedures to maintain integrity of assessment device.   **Y**   **N**
Comments:

The learner has sufficient background and understanding of assessment to
successfully complete the testing device.   **Y**   **N**
Comments:

Assessment accommodations are implemented to account for second language
acquisition needs of the student.   **Y**   **N**
Comments:

Learner possesses sufficient English skills to successfully complete the test if
it is administered in English.   **Y**   **N**
Comments:

Learner is provided opportunity to become familiar with the format of the device
prior to test completion (e.g., short answer, multiple choice, true-false).   **Y**   **N**
Comments:

Instrument's manual discusses appropriate uses of the device with culturally
and linguistically diverse learners.   **Y**   **N**
Comments:

Form 8.3   Checklist for Effective Assessment of Diverse Learners

Student: _____ Date: _____

Assessment Team Members: _____

Effective assessment for culturally/linguistically diverse learners includes attention to the following ten educational areas:

1. Instructional Components
2. Prereferral Interventions
3. Cultural/Linguistic Prereferral Considerations
4. Diagnostic Assessment
5. Decision-Making Process
6. Difference Versus Disability Clarification
7. Student Cultural/Linguistic Factors
8. Consideration of Classroom Factors
9. Consideration of Home/Community Factors
10. Language Proficiency Assessment

Instructions: Check each item within the educational area once it is addressed in the multi-tiered assessment process.

1. Instructional Components: The following instructional considerations have been confirmed through various assessment practices (e.g., observations, interviews, work sample analysis):

____ Sufficient opportunities to learn in Tiers 1 and 2

____ Scaffolding of instruction

____ Instruction in primary language

____ Functional, purposeful conversations

____ Cooperative, shared activities

____ Sufficient "wait" time for student response

____ Student's prior knowledge activated and valued

____ Instruction reflective of learner's cultural and linguistic background

2. Prereferral Opportunities: The following exist *prior to* a formal referral is made and *before* formal assessment is initiated:

____ Documentation of the instructional components (above) occurs.

____ Cultural factors related to suspected area of need are identified.

____ Tier 1 instruction is provided in culturally/linguistically competent ways.

____ Tier 2 supplemental instruction is provided in culturally/linguistically competent ways.

____ Progress-monitoring results are documented.

____ Evidence-based interventions are implemented.

Form 8.3 (Continued)

3. Cultural/Linguistic Prereferral Considerations: Various alternative explanations for the exhibited behaviors are explored including cultural/linguistic explanations for:

___ Extended periods of silence

___ Confusion with locus of control

___ Withdrawal

___ Low self-esteem

___ Increased anxiety

___ Difficulty observing school/class rules or expectations

___ Difficulty completing assignments in a timely manner

___ Length of wait time needed to respond to questions/tasks

4. Diagnostic Assessment: The following exist in the assessment of a culturally/linguistically diverse learner:

___ Assessment occurs in primary language, and English, if bilingual.

___ A variety of assessment practices are completed (e.g., observations, interviews, curriculum-based measurement, etc.) in addition to diagnostic testing.

___ Translators/interpreters are properly used.

___ Learner possesses sufficient experiential background to complete assessment tasks and instruments.

___ Assessment devices contain sufficient norming data to demonstrate effectiveness with ELLs.

___ Assessment practices are implemented in culturally and linguistically responsive ways (e.g., CBM, task analysis, performance-based assessment, etc.).

___ Review of records and home language survey are completed.

___ Valid assessment devices are used.

___ Valid assessment process is followed.

___ Overall nondiscriminatory assessment is conducted.

___ Suspected need is considered relative to:

___ conversational and academic language levels

___ acculturation needs

___ experiential background

___ cultural values and norms

___ compatibility between teaching style and preferred student learning styles (e.g., group versus individual, competitive versus cooperative, etc.)

___ higher order thinking abilities emphasized

5. Decision-Making Process: The following exist to ensure unbiased decision making:

___ All appropriate people are involved in assessment and eligibility decisions (e.g., bilingual/ESL educator, speech/language specialist, general/special class teacher, social worker, parents, assessment specialist, etc.).

___ Culturally responsive process for making instructional and eligibility decisions is adhered to when considering an ELL for possible special education.

____ Results and recommendations from team decisions are documented and justified.

____ Discussions about culturally and linguistically diverse factors occur prior to the decisions made.

6. Difference Versus Disability Clarification: The following are confirmed to clarify difference from disability:

____ Problems with learning exist in both languages/cultures.

____ Academic/behavioral difficulties exist over extended period of time despite implementation of culturally/linguistically appropriate interventions.

____ Need area requires intensive interventions.

____ Unbiased assessment practices/devices are used and indicate a suspected disability.

____ Concerns associated with cognitive abilities are evident in both languages/cultures.

7. Student Cultural/Linguistic Factors: The following are addressed and considered in the overall assessment of the suspected area of need:

____ Communicative and academic language levels

____ Level and effects of acculturation

____ Experiential background

____ Cultural values/norms

____ Use of higher order thinking abilities

8. Consideration of Classroom Factors: The following exist in the classroom and instructional environment:

____ Higher-order instructional tasks and thinking abilities encouraged in the curriculum and instruction

____ Compatibility between teaching and learning styles

____ Joint productive classroom activities (i.e., interactions among students, teacher)

____ Active, ongoing verbal dialogue

____ Cultural values/norms incorporated into the curriculum and instruction

9. Consideration of Home/Community Factors: The following are addressed and considered in the overall assessment of the suspected area of need:

____ Adjustments to new community environments

____ Home language

____ Language most used with peers

____ Educational history

10. Language Proficiency Assessment

____ Most proficient language is determined prior to referral or completion of formal assessment.

____ Opportunities to learn reflect instruction in most proficient language.

9

Future Challenges in RTI Assessment

SIGNIFICANCE TO CONTEMPORARY ASSESSMENT

As more and more school systems implement multi-tiered response to intervention models, many of the initial assessment challenges will be overcome and, hopefully, needs of struggling learners will be met under more preventative conditions. However, some assessment challenges will continue to exist and grow, and the next level of discussion concerning multi-tiered response to intervention must focus on particulars that affect several key areas: collaboration, time, training, support, diversity, fidelity, and validity. While these aspects are addressed on a general level by school systems as initial efforts to implement multi-tiered instruction occur, each will continue to challenge most educators as core, supplemental, and intensive interventions are implemented and assessed. The significance of considering these continuing challenges is found in the need to successfully account for each element of support to ensure the sustainable, long-term implementation of effective RTI assessment.

CHAPTER OVERVIEW

Chapter 9 provides discussion and consideration of several key elements directly associated with the successful implementation of assessments conducted within multi-tiered RTI. Several recurring issues in education that must be addressed are discussed. Overall, these relate to the collaborative efforts necessary to meet all needs of struggling learners in today's classrooms.

Key Topics Addressed in Chapter

Assessment challenges related to:

- ✦ Significance of Collaboration
- ✦ Efficient Time Management
- ✦ Necessary Professional Development and Training
- ✦ Ongoing Assessment Support
- ✦ Meeting Diverse Needs
- ✦ Maintaining Fidelity
- ✦ Assessment Validity

LEARNER OUTCOMES

Upon completion of Chapter 9 readers will

- acquire a greater understanding for the need to continue personal professional development within RTI
- be more prepared to address multi-tiered assessment issues in the future
- become more informed of continuing assessment challenges facing all educators in multi-tiered instruction
- acquire more proficiency in abilities to ask appropriate questions to best meet assessment fidelity and validity needs for struggling learners

PERSONAL PERSPECTIVE

The education of learners occurs in a fluid and dynamic structure where existing knowledge about best practices, assessment procedures, decision-making processes, and disabilities continues to evolve. Among the many changes I have seen over the past several decades, few have had more of a significant impact on teachers and their students than the increased emphasis on assessment and associated accountability. A prevailing challenge for us all as we attempt to provide the best education possible to struggling learners is that of continued professional development to remain up-to-date with the most current educational assessment practices and devices. Today, we see a significant emphasis being placed on assessment as it relates directly to instruction, rather than assessment to determine deficits within individuals.

I believe that high-quality teaching requires us to continue moving forward in addressing current challenges. The topics addressed in this chapter provide a summary of some of the issues I have seen in my recent work within multi-tiered response to intervention and in assessment over the past few decades. Meeting

(Continued)

(Continued)

the needs of struggling learners requires educators to continually assess progress and make necessary instructional adjustments. Our challenge is to continue to evaluate our efforts, our decision making, and our results to best assess and meet the academic and social-emotional needs of all struggling learners educated within multi-tiered response to intervention models.

CONFRONTING CONTINUING CHALLENGES

Most educators understand that the successful implementation of multi-tiered response to intervention requires: (1) additional emphasis in some areas, (2) addition of new instructional components, and (3) the need to discontinue certain educational practices embedded in our school systems over the past several decades. Therefore, recognition that the implementation of multi-tiered instruction requires change further supports the need for ongoing professional development in several key assessment areas. While not all-inclusive, several important assessment factors continue to challenge both educators and struggling learners. This book concludes with a brief overview of selected assessment issues along with suggestions to continue to address them in productive ways.

Assessment Challenge 1: Collaboration

In no area of our schools is the need for collaboration among general and special educators more pronounced than in our efforts to implement assessment within multi-tiered response to intervention. Stated simply, few individual or pairs of educators possess a sufficient amount of knowledge and expertise to meet all assessment needs of the many diverse learners found in today's classrooms. Whether it be a language, reading, mathematics, behavioral, attention, concept thinking, or some other educational challenge, educators must collaborate to screen, monitor, and, if necessary, diagnose needs related to academic and social-emotional progress of struggling learners. While different educators must take the lead in completing various assessments, others must be willing to collaborate to help address many of the other factors that potentially interfere with accurate and valid assessment (e.g., sufficient time, expertise, training).

Facilitating Collaboration

Assessment teams and processes should be structured to facilitate collaboration among different educators to successfully help each other meet the demands associated with multi-tiered RTI models. If collaboration is built into the process from its inception, it will have a better chance of being implemented and succeeding.

Assessment Challenge 2: Time

"I would really like to do that, but I don't have the time." How often have we said or heard this in our various meetings and conversations about what to do with struggling learners? Most educators genuinely want to help struggling learners if provided sufficient time to implement necessary instruction and associated assessments. One fact concerning multi-tiered instructional assessment is that more educators must share in the responsibilities to collect and document assessment results. Specifically, educators are challenged with the need to conduct short and quick ongoing assessments to monitor progress on a more continuous basis, rather than waiting until year's end to determine student progress. This introduces the need for more efficient management of time within classroom instruction.

Restructuring Classroom Management

Teachers who structure the management of their classrooms in a manner that anticipates learner needs and potential problems prior to their occurrence are more successful at helping learners assume increased responsibility for their own learning and behaviors. Restructuring classroom management to allow students to assume more responsibility, in turn, provides the teacher more time for other instructional or assessment tasks. This increase in time within the classroom may not be substantial; however, for many teachers, it will provide sufficient restructuring of time to complete the added progress-monitoring requirements associated with multi-tiered response to intervention models. The less time teachers do things "for" students and the more time teachers "allow" students to do things for themselves the greater the flexibility in time management within classrooms.

Assessment Challenge 3: Training and Professional Development

As discussed, multi-tiered response to intervention has created a new or different emphasis on assessment associated with classroom instruction. As a result, all educators require training to best implement necessary changes and to remain current with preferred and best practices, along with new or increased assessment roles. While many school systems are providing some of the necessary training, ongoing development must continue for most educators to further enhance and refine their RTI assessment abilities. Becoming proficient with the selection, administration, reporting, and interpretation of universal screening, progress monitoring, and diagnostic assessment is critical to effective multi-tiered response to intervention and requires continued professional development and training.

Develop a Personal Professional Development Plan

Educators should self-evaluate skills and abilities possessed to currently meet the most critical aspects of RTI assessment such as management of time, collaboration, procedures for administering and charting assessment results, or understanding the connection between that which is assessed and what is taught—to name a few. This should be followed by the development of a personal professional development plan where the goal is to increase the knowledge, skills, and expertise in all aspects of assessment in multi-tiered instruction that most directly affect one's individual role. Included in this plan should be the documentation of activities to meet this goal along with a timeline. Activities such as coursework, workshops, conferences, or district trainings should be considered. Overall, a personal professional development plan completed over a reasonable amount of time will provide educators with the knowledge and expertise to successfully implement necessary assessments as well as demonstrate to others that the assessments are conducted with fidelity.

Assessment Challenge 4: Team Support

As discussed in previous chapters, each school has some form of assessment team that provides direction, expertise, and support for multi-tiered instructional decisions based on screening, monitoring, or diagnostic results. Along with professional development and associated training, educators must receive ongoing support from others on the multi-tiered assessment teams. Ongoing support serves at least three important purposes: (1) increases confidence in teachers that assessments are being conducted properly, (2) allows colleagues to corroborate that assessments are completed with fidelity, and (3) maintains the integrity of collaboration among team members given the wide variety of areas of expertise required to meet assessment needs of all struggling learners.

Build a Strong Assessment Team

The most efficient way to ensure that ongoing team support is provided to all educators is to build this support into the structure of the assessment team as it is being formed. Should the team already be formed, then a restructuring should occur, if necessary, to best support ongoing collaboration to assist teachers with multi-tiered assessment requirements. This includes ensuring that the proper personnel are on the assessment team as well as conducting effective meetings within established timelines. Support from team members may take the form of consultation, observation, or direct administration of assessments. If these tasks are designed to assist educators to do their work more effectively, an increase in valid assessment results will be obtained.

Assessment Challenge 5: Diversity

Chapter 8 of this book discussed some of the key issues associated with the implementation of multi-tiered instruction with diverse learners, highlighting the need to: (1) reduce the perpetuation of problematic practices, (2) increase personal development of culturally responsive education and assessment, and (3) provide diverse learners sufficient opportunities to learn. The challenge to meet diverse needs in assessment has existed for decades and continues to be an issue due to misunderstandings or misinterpretations of learning differences as disabilities. In addition, as districts continue to attempt to require identical assessments for all learners, the needs of diverse learners may be compromised due to cultural and linguistic diversity brought to the classroom environment and assessment situation.

Increase Cultural Proficiency

All educators must become familiar with current problematic practices that lead to erroneous assessment decisions for diverse learners as well as provide leadership to reduce these practices within the multi-tiered assessment team structure. Additionally, meeting this challenge requires all educators to self-evaluate their cultural proficiency in teaching and assessment and develop a plan to increase personal skills. Strategies to meet this challenge could easily be included in one's personal professional development plan previously described.

Assessment Challenge 6: Fidelity

The importance of integrity in assessment cannot be overstated since, if fidelity does not exist, assessment scores are suspect and may easily lead to misplacement or selection of an inappropriate tier of intervention. Therefore, a continuing challenge facing all educators pertains to fidelity in the selection, implementation, scoring, and uses of assessment results to best meet struggling learners' needs. As previously discussed, fidelity of assessment begins with the proper selection of the correct instrument or practice that reflects reliability and validity for use with the intended population of students, followed by the proper implementation of the selected device or practice. This, in turn, is followed by proper interpretation and uses of the assessment scores or results, maintaining integrity by only using results in ways they were researched and intended for use. The accuracy of assessment results is of utmost concern in multi-tiered response to intervention given the significance placed upon assessment scores to base instructional and diagnostic decisions. Therefore, a continuing challenge is to ensure that each aspect of the RTI assessment process is completed properly and fairly for all struggling learners.

Get Familiar With Assessment's Proper Implementation

The ability to maintain fidelity in assessment begins with possessing the knowledge needed to best understand the assessment devices or practices being used with struggling learners. This includes acquiring a working knowledge of the assessment's purpose, intended uses, procedures, reliability, validity, and appropriateness for use with the population of learners. Therefore, to best meet this assessment challenge, educators should become familiar with these aspects of the assessment devices or practices used in universal screening, progress monitoring, or diagnostic to empower themselves in being able to successfully complete required assessments with fidelity.

Assessment Challenge 7: Validity

Ultimately, the validity of assessment determines its appropriateness for use with the intended struggling learners. The extent to which any aspect of the assessment process is invalid is the extent to which the uses or applications of the assessment results become invalid. Given the widespread emphasis of assessment throughout the entire multi-tiered RTI process, educators must continuously evaluate the validity of the assessment process. This includes validity related to the device or practice, procedures for implementing the device or practice, scoring of results, as well as decisions concerning the level and intensity of instruction based on those results.

Check Validity Throughout All RTI Tiers

To best meet this assessment challenge, all educators must assume the responsibility to ensure assessment validity. Those selecting assessment devices/practices must ensure they are valid for their intended purposes; those implementing the assessment devices/practices must ensure that they are completed as designed; and those interpreting and using the assessment results must ensure that they are used in ways they are designed to be used, avoiding using results outside intended purposes. Maintaining assessment validity challenges all educators on multi-tiered RTI assessment teams, and the validity must be re-evaluated each time critical instructional or eligibility decisions are made for struggling learners.

SUMMARY

Throughout this book, many of the most pressing issues, concerns, and needs associated with multi-tiered response to intervention assessment have been presented. This includes a focus on the assessment continuum of screening, progress monitoring, and diagnostic for struggling learners who bring a variety of diverse needs to the instructional environment. This chapter highlighted some of the most current issues and needs that will continue to challenge all educators in our attempts to identify early and prevent academic or behavior problems from becoming more severe. As these challenges are continuously addressed in the future, the education of all struggling students will improve by providing learners with timely, valid, and informed assessment. This, in turn, provides the best opportunity for multi-tiered response to intervention to be improved and maintained for all students who struggle in today's educational environments.

Applying Chapter 9 Learning Outcomes

1. Evaluate your preparation to make informed and valid assessment decisions in each aspect of the assessment continuum: universal screening, progress monitoring, and diagnostic.

2. Develop a personal professional development plan with a colleague to cooperatively increase knowledge and skills in the assessment challenge areas discussed in this chapter.

3. Select and implement one assessment practice (e.g., CBM, task analysis, performance-based) that you are least familiar with to increase your assessment skills and knowledge.

4. Design and implement a PowerPoint presentation for your school's faculty discussing some of the most critical issues challenging your school in the successful implementation of your multi-tiered RTI model.

Appendix

PowerPoint Presentation—
RTI Assessment and Struggling Learners

AN INTRODUCTORY OVERVIEW

The following training PowerPoint/overhead slides are presented for trainers to use in their professional development for colleagues. This presentation provides an introductory overview of the primary topics, issues, and concepts covered in this book to introduce the topic of RTI assessment essentials in multi-tiered response to intervention for struggling learners.

RTI Assessment and
Struggling Learners
by
John J. Hoover, PhD

Presentation based on the material found in:

RTI Assessment Essentials for Struggling Learners by John J. Hoover

Overview of Presentation

Section I: Overview of Multi-Tiered RTI
              Continuum of Assessment
              Ecological Factors in RTI Assessment

****

Section II: Assessment Fidelity
              Evidence-Based Assessment
              RTI and Special Education

****

Section III: Decision-Making Process
              Difference From Disability
              Future Assessment Challenges

Section I - Part 1

Presentation Goal:

Acquire Overview of Multi-Tiered
Response to Intervention

Multi-Tiered Response to Intervention (RTI)

Educational Concerns

1) Educational practices often used in the classroom lack a research base to justify use to meet purported needs.

2) Educational practices are appropriate to meet purported needs but are not implemented in a manner in which they were developed, therefore lacking implementation with fidelity.

Multi-Tiered Response to Intervention (RTI)

Tier	Description
1 - Core	Implementation of research-based curriculum for all learners in the general classroom.
2 - Supplemental	Implementation of instruction that supplements the Tier 1 core such as small group instruction to provide targeted support.
3 - Intensive	Implementation of specialized interventions to meet more significant needs, including special education.

Multi-Tiered Assessment Implications

Multi-tiered response to intervention has direct assessment implications for struggling learners:

1. Implementation of evidence-based interventions must occur prior to conducting response to intervention assessment.

2. Use of research-based assessment practices is necessary to adequately determine response to instruction.

Multi-Tiered Assessment Implications

3. Interventions must be implemented in the classroom in the manner in which they were researched and validated prior to making judgments that a student is struggling in school.

4. If appropriate evidence-based instruction is not provided to a struggling learner, it must be implemented prior to gathering and using assessment data to make instructional decisions.

5. Collection of frequent and regular assessment data reflecting student progress forms the foundation for basing decisions about the level and intensity of instruction a learner should receive.

Section I - Part 2

Presentation Goal:

Understand Continuum of Assessment in RTI

Assessment Continuum

Universal Screening	Progress Monitoring	Diagnostic Assessment
Tier 1	Tiers 1/2/3	Tiers 2/3

Multi-Tiered Assessment

Universal Screening

Practice by which all students are screened (usually three times per year), to determine level of attainment of district curricular benchmarks for the purpose of identifying struggling learners.

Multi-Tiered Assessment

Progress Monitoring

Task of systematically gathering assessment data to determine the extent to which a student responds to evidence-based instruction by monitoring progress on a frequent basis (e.g., monthly, weekly, daily), based on level or tier of instruction provided.

Multi-Tiered Assessment

Diagnostic Assessment

Type of specialized assessment by which individual learning needs are diagnosed to make informed decisions concerning potential special education placement and eligibility or related intensive interventions.

Competencies for Assessment Continuum

Effective implementation of assessments along the continuum requires educators to

- understand purpose
- see connection to classroom instruction
- include procedures for proper implementation
- understand fidelity in implementation
- accurately chart results
- properly interpret results
- apply scores in valid ways
- understand types of decisions made from results

Section I - Part 3

Presentation Goal:

Acquire Understanding of Ecologically Responsive Assessment

Ecological Framework in Multi-Tiered RTI

An ecological assessment framework reflective of the student's total environment is considered relative to teaching and learning needs.

A major premise of ecological theory is that a student exists and develops within a broader context that includes home and community as well as the classroom (Bronfenbrenner, 1995).

Factors in Ecological Framework

Student Factors

Refers to elements such as experiential background and prior educational experiences. Also includes consideration of student's preferred styles of learning (e.g., cooperative versus independent, study of the whole versus discrete parts) as well as emphasis on use of higher order thinking skills in learning (e.g., synthesis, evaluation, comprehension).

Factors in Ecological Framework

Classroom Factors

Ysseldyke and Christenson (2002) identified several classroom instructional factors that contribute to an ecological perspective in education. These include instructional expectations, feedback, academic learning time, adaptations, and strategies for motivation.

Factors in Ecological Framework

Home/Community Factors

Factors such as cultural values and norms, views toward education, preferences toward learning, or adjustment to new environments are some of the home/community factors to consider (Hoover, Klingner et al., 2008).

Ecologically Responsive Assessment

Since assessment decisions provide the basis for determining the most appropriate level of intervention for all learners in multi-tiered response to intervention, assessment teams must incorporate key ecological factors in the process to make the most informed decisions possible.

Ecological Validity- Cohen (1995) described ecological validity in research as a practice that allows researchers to describe and evaluate how real people operate in the real world.

Ecologically Responsive Assessment Summary

- Three ecological factors (i.e., student, classroom, home/community) must be adequately and meaningfully addressed in the assessment process.
- Ecological validity must exist to best incorporate environmental influences in the interpretation of and inferences made from assessment scores.
- Tiered progress-monitoring procedures must be selected in consideration of the various ecological factors to meet needs of all struggling learners.

Section II - Part 1

Presentation Goal:

Acquire Knowledge About
Fidelity of Assessment

Assessment Fidelity

Fidelity of assessment in multi-tiered response to intervention refers to

- proper implementation of the assessment practices, procedures, and devices
- accurately drawing proper inferences from obtained assessment scores
- simultaneous consideration of ecological factors of student, school/classroom, and home/community to best explain and apply assessment results

Assessment Fidelity

Fidelity requires that

1) The assessment device and/or practice is implemented according to the validated procedures discussed in the manual or related write-up.

2) The obtained assessment scores are used for purposes consistent with the way they are recommended to be used as determined through the validity studies.

3) Ecological factors are considered to ensure the most appropriate and informed decision making occurs.

Fidelity in Implementing Assessment Devices

All credible assessment devices possess evidence of high reliability and validity.

In order to implement assessment devices with fidelity, educators must be knowledgeable about several factors including the following:

- population included in its research and development
- standardized procedures for properly administering the device
- prerequisite administration skills of the administrator
- recommended setting for administration
- time allotments necessary for proper administration

Fidelity in Implementing Assessment Practices

Similar to the implementation of assessment devices, every assessment practice must be implemented with fidelity to yield accurate results.

Assessment practices contain certain steps or procedures to follow for proper implementation and these must be adhered to for accurate results.

Fidelity in Implementing Assessment Accommodations

Assessment accommodations are acceptable practices that assist in the implementation of fair and unbiased assessment.

These may include accommodations in time, setting, schedule, response mode, and presentation.

Fidelity in the implementation of assessment accommodations must include ensuring that only the assessment conditions are manipulated and not that which is being assessed.

Fidelity in Use of Assessment Scores

Ultimately, fidelity of assessment is seen in the proper interpretation and uses of assessment results to make well-informed instructional or diagnostic decisions:

Assessment scores or results that are generated from an assessment process that lacks fidelity yield assessment decisions that in turn lack integrity, credibility, and value to those students for which critical decisions are being made in multi-tiered instruction.

Section II - Part 2

Presentation Goal:

Acquire an Overview of Evidence-Based Assessment Practices

Curriculum-Based Measurement

Curriculum-based measurement (CBM) is an assessment practice that provides educators with "reliable, valid and efficient indicators of academic competence" (Fuchs & Fuchs, 2007, p. 31).

Curriculum-Based Measurement

Curriculum-based measurement:

a) directly assesses that which has been taught
b) records quantified performance data over time
c) is completed quickly in a less time-consuming manner due to process of several short assessments implemented over time, rather than one longer assessment completed at only one point in time
d) provides a structure for educators to acquire, record, chart, and share student performance data in standard ways so all involved may easily evaluate the quality of instruction provided and make necessary changes as indicated

Analytic Teaching

An evidence-based assessment practice that provides educators a systematic structure to observe student progress and learning behaviors by subdividing tasks as necessary (Baca & Cervantes, 2004).

Analytic Teaching

Key Points . . .

- documents student strengths and struggling areas in learning
- provides educators information about the manner in which learners complete instructional activities
- assists in forming hypotheses of the student needs
- identifies needed steps to successfully complete tasks
- progress monitors student responses to instructional activities
- uses higher order thinking abilities in assessment
- allows complex tasks to be more easily broken down for struggling learners
- integrates instruction with assessment and monitoring of progress
- allows preferred styles of learning to be identified and observed

Interviews/Observations

Interviews - Useful assessment practice to clarify a variety of student academic and social/emotional needs, strengths, behaviors, or preferences with current and former teachers, parents, peers, and other significant others in the student's life.

Observations - Classroom practice to provide corroborating evidence to support, refute, or further clarify data gathered from use of other assessment practices.

Work Sample Analysis

Educators are provided with specific examples, over time, of actual student work in targeted academic or behavioral areas.

Using a rubric to quantify various aspects of student work provides additional information to support progress-monitoring efforts.

As work sample analysis data are charted over time, along with other progress data, a more in-depth and complete picture of student work in various content/behavioral areas is illustrated.

Task Analysis

Task analysis provides a process for identifying specific procedures and prerequisites necessary for task completion (Hallahan et al., 2005).

When implemented properly, task analysis assists to identify skills a student has mastered and those requiring additional support in order to best complete a task.

The sequential process associated with task analysis provides educators a structured framework within which multi-tiered response to instruction decisions may be made.

Performance-Based and Functional-Based Assessments

Performance-Based: assessment where learner performance is evaluated based on a comprehensive student-constructed response or product (Bender, 2002).

Functional-Based: assessment where the conditions associated with inappropriate behaviors are identified in order to develop a plan to reduce the occurrence of that behavior (Kirk, Gallagher, & Anastasiow, 2006).

Running Records

A form of miscue analysis for use with learners struggling with reading that is easy to implement, generating recorded data (Clay, 1993).

When running records are completed over time, the charted data (i.e., number of correctly read words in ten-minute block of time) illustrate student progress.

Assessment Accommodations

- *Presentation.* The manner in which material is presented is modified such as more or less reliance on visual or auditory presentation.
- *Response.* The manner in which the student is required to respond to assessment items is altered.
- *Time.* The time provided to allow the learner to respond to the assessment items is adjusted to allow for more accurate response.
- *Scheduling.* In some instances, the test taking schedule should be altered (e.g., breaking the test taking into different segments, offering at a more appropriate time of the day).
- *Setting.* The location in which the assessment is completed may need to be changed to a different classroom or other location in the school building (e.g., library).

Section II - Part 3

Presentation Goal:

Understand Role of RTI in
Special Education

Role of RTI in the Special
Education Process

Students in multi-tiered instruction may eventually be referred for special education consideration (Vaughn, 2003).

If a persistent lack of progress is demonstrated after continuous monitoring of progress, a formal referral to special education may be warranted (Tier 3).

Prereferral and RTI

For students who eventually are referred to special education within multi-tiered response to intervention, supplemental and intensive interventions become, in effect, prereferral interventions, with all assessment results important in the special education eligibility decision-making process.

Assessing Opportunities to Learn

The following need to be determined in the assessment of opportunities to learn (Hoover, Klingner et al., 2008):

- experiential background with the assessment/instruction
- proficiency of language of assessment/instruction
- student perception of relevancy of assessment/instruction
- sufficient time to complete instructional activities and associated assessment
- assessment accommodations (if necessary)
- relationship between that which is being assessed and that which was taught
- sufficient adjustments to instruction
- uses of valid assessment devices/practices relative to assessed areas

Assessing Opportunities to Learn

All learners considered for eligibility for special education must be provided sufficient opportunities to learn the content and skills related to the suspected disability area.

Special Educator Role in RTI

Participation on the part of special educators across all tiers facilitates providing:

- consultative assistance to general educators in identifying appropriate assessment accommodations
- opportunity for special educators to begin to acquire an understanding of the struggling learner early in the screening and monitoring process, rather than waiting until the problem becomes more severe

Special Educator Role in RTI

Participation on the part of special educators across all tiers facilitates providing:

- expertise in a variety of classroom management interventions that may assist with the integration of instruction with progress monitoring
- collaborative efforts in attempting to meet struggling learner needs identified through the classroom-based assessments
- targeted efforts to avoid the previous assessment practice in which special educators only became involved after general education efforts failed, perpetuating the "wait to fail" process before special education knowledge and expertise are solicited

Section III - Part 1

Presentation Goal:

Develop Multi-Tiered
Instructional Problem-Solving Skills

Multi-Tiered Assessment Decisions

Multi-tiered RTI helps educators make critical decisions related to

- extent to which the learner is meeting curricular benchmarks/objectives (includes both rate of progress and level of meeting targeted objectives)
- tier (of intervention) to provide to the learner, based on data demonstrating progress toward meeting benchmarks/objectives
- effectiveness of evidence-based interventions on student progress (i.e., RTI)
- eligibility for formal special education assessment and/or placement for a disability

Standard Treatment Protocol Model

This model provides similar forms of interventions and assessment for all learners who experience the same need (e.g., reading fluency).

Through standard treatment protocol, decisions are based on the progress-monitoring data and charted over time; this is considered more accurate in identifying "children truly in need of special services" (Fuchs & Fuchs, 2006, p. 97) than other approaches.

Problem-Solving Model

This model is less rigorous than the standard treatment method in that it relies on a variety of factors and educator input to make decisions, rather than primarily relying on only standard assessment data.

However, as Fuchs and Fuchs (2006) point out, this method assists to ensure that "all children with special needs receive appropriate services" (p. 97) and therefore is a more inclusive model, yet runs the risk of incorrectly perceiving special needs when in reality they do not exist.

Standard Treatment
Problem-Solving Model

This combined model includes elements found in both the standard treatment and traditional problem-solving models.

The combined model focuses on data derived from ongoing progress monitoring as the foundation for decision making, yet it also provides for inclusion and consideration of other related factors to best understand the complete situation.

Assessment Team Members

Potential Members of Multi-Tiered Response to Intervention Assessment Decision-Making Teams:

- General Class Teacher
- Special Educator
- Assessment Specialist (e.g., School Psychologist)
- Content Area Specialist
- ESL/Bilingual Educator
- Speech/Language Specialist
- Behavioral Specialist (may include Social Worker)
- Parents/Guardians
- Paraprofessional
- Other

Section III - Part 2

Presentation Goal:

Distinguish Between Learning
Differences and Disabilities

Differences and Similarities in Education

Differences REQUIRE that we vary what we do with learners.

Similarities REFLECT that all or some groups of students learn best in similar ways.

Attempting to implement similarities in education for learners with *differences* causes:

- significant conflicts
- ineffective instruction
- erroneous assessment decisions

Differences in Education

The single biggest error made in placing diverse learners into special education is . . .

misinterpreting a learning or language difference as a learning or language disability.

Assessment teams must become better at making this distinction.

Problematic Practices

Several educational practices perpetuate misinterpretation of learning differences as disabilities:

- lack of exposure to multicultural perspectives (*educator issue*)
- failure to incorporate cultural values/norms in the curriculum (*relevance issue*)
- language differences are misunderstood as language/reading disabilities (*diagnosis issue*)
- failure to accommodate acculturation (*cultural issue*)

Problematic Practices

Educational practices perpetuating misinterpretation of learning differences as disabilities (continued):

- lack of inclusion of both first and second languages (*language issue*)
- insufficient opportunities to learn (*instructional issue*)
- biased assessment (*assessment issue*)

Preferred Practices

- Learner is provided sufficient opportunities in the assessment process to demonstrate acquired knowledge and skills.
- The implementation of appropriate evidence-based assessment is done in culturally-responsive ways.
- Assessment reflects challenging tasks including emphasis on higher-level tasks.
- Assessment accounts for acculturation needs.
- Assessment is conducted in the most proficient language and/or English.
- Assessment practices are compatible with preferred ways of learning consistent with cultural values/norms.
- Assessment is implemented by culturally competent educator.
- Unbiased assessment is completed with fidelity.

Section III - Part 3

Presentation Goal:

Identify Future
Assessment Challenges

Assessment Challenges

Several aspects continue to challenge educators in multi-tiered instructional assessment:

- significance of collaboration
- efficient time management
- necessary professional development and training
- ongoing assessment support
- meeting diverse needs
- maintaining fidelity
- assessment validity

Assessment Challenges: *Looking Forward*

As these challenges are continuously addressed in the future, the education of all struggling learners will improve by providing them with timely, valid, and informed assessment.

References

Alper, S., Ryndak, D. L., & Schloss, C. N. (2001). *Alternate assessment of students with disabilities in inclusive settings.* Boston: Allyn & Bacon.

Baca, L., & Cervantes, H. T. (2004). *The bilingual special education interface.* Columbus, OH: Merrill.

Bender, W. N. (2002). *Differentiating instruction for students with learning disabilities: Best teaching practices for general and special educators.* Thousand Oaks, CA: Corwin Press.

Bender, W. N., & Shores, C. (2007). *Response to intervention: A practical guide for every teacher.* Thousand Oaks, CA: Corwin Press.

Bronfenbrenner, U. (1979). *The ecology of human development.* Cambridge, MA: Harvard University Press.

Bronfenbrenner, U. (1995). Developmental ecology through space and time: A future perspective. In P. Moen, G. Elder, & K. Leuscher (Eds.), *Examining lives in context: Perspectives on the ecology of human development* (pp. 619–647). Washington, DC: American Psychological Association.

Bronfenbrenner, U. (Ed.) (2005). *Making human beings human: Ecological perspectives on human development.* Thousand Oaks, CA: Sage Publications.

Brown, L. (2004). Evaluating and managing classroom behavior. In D. D. Hammill & N. R. Bartel, *Teaching students with learning and behavior problems* (pp. 255–290). Austin, TX: PRO-ED.

Brown-Chidsey, R., & Steege, M. W. (2005). *Response to intervention: Principles and strategies for effective practice.* New York: Guilford Press.

Carroll, J. B. (1963). A model of school learning. *Teachers College Record, 64,* 723–733.

Clay, M. (1993). *Reading recovery: A guidebook for teachers in training.* Portsmouth, NH: Heinemann.

Cohen, L. G., & Spenciner, L. J. (2007). *Assessment of children and youth with special needs.* Boston: Pearson.

Cohen, P. R. (1995). *Ecological validity: Making experiments relevant.* Retrieved February 10, 2008, from http://www.cs.colostate.edu/~howe/EMAI/ch3/node18.html.

Collier, V. P., & Thomas, W. P. (1989). How quickly can immigrants become proficient in English? *Journal of Educational Issues of Language Minority Students, 5,* 25–38.

Colorado Department of Education (CDE) (2008). *Response to intervention (RtI): A practitioner's guide to implementation.* Denver, CO: Colorado Department of Education. Author.

Compton, D. L., Fuchs, D., Fuchs, L. S., & Bryant, J. D. (2006). Selecting at-risk readers in first grade for early intervention: A two-year longitudinal study of decision rules and procedures. *Journal of Educational Psychology, 98,* 394–409.

Council for Exceptional Children (CEC) (2008). CEC's position on response to intervention (RTI): Unique role of special education and special educators. *Teaching Exceptional Children,* Jan/Feb, 74–75.

Crone, D. A., & Horner, R. H. (2003). *Building positive behavior support systems in schools: Functional behavioral assessment.* New York: Guilford Press.

Deno, S. L. (1985). Curriculum-based measurement: The emerging alternative. *Exceptional Children, 52,* 219–232.

Deno, S. L. (2005). Problem-solving assessment. In R. Brown-Chidsey (Ed.), *Assessment for intervention: A problem-solving approach* (pp. 10–40). New York: Guilford Press.

Durand, V. M., & Carr, E. G., (1985). Self-injurious behavior: Motivating conditions and guidelines for treatment. *School Psychology Review, 14* (2), 171–176.

Eisner, E. W. (2002). *The educational imagination: On design and evaluation of school programs* (3rd ed.). Columbus, OH: Merrill/Prentice Hall.

Fuchs, D., & Fuchs, L. S. (2007). The role of assessment in the three-tier approach to reading instruction. In D. Haager, J. Klingner, & S. Vaughn (Eds.), *Evidence-based reading practices for response to intervention* (pp. 29–42). Baltimore, MD: Brookes Publishing.

Fuchs, L. S. (2003). Assessing intervention responsiveness: Conceptual and technical issues. *Learning Disabilities Research and Practice, 18* (3), 172–186.

Fuchs, D., & Fuchs, L. S. (2006). Introduction to response to intervention: What, why, and how valid is it? *Reading Research Quarterly, 41* (1), 95–99.

Gacka, R. C. (2006). *Learning differences fast facts.* Retrieved May 17, 2008, from Pennsylvania Adult Basic and Literacy Education (ABLE) web site: http://www.pde.state.pa.us/able/cwp/view.asp?a=15&q=121698.

Gay, G. (2000). *Culturally responsive teaching.* New York: Teachers College Press.

Goh, D. S. (2004). *Assessment accommodations for diverse learners.* Boston: Pearson.

Haager, D., Klingner, J., & Vaughn, S. (2007). *Evidence-based reading practices for response to intervention.* Baltimore: Brookes Publishing.

Hallahan, D. P., Lloyd, J., Kauffman, J. M., Weiss, M. P., & Martinez, E. A. (2005). *Learning disabilities: Foundations, characteristics, and effective teaching* (3rd ed.). Boston: Pearson.

Hoover, J. J. (2006). *Framework for implementing culturally competent response to intervention* (Invited Presentation). Summit on Differentiated Instruction and Academic Intervention. New York: NYC Public Schools, April 25, 2006.

Hoover, J. J. (2008). Data-driven decision making in a multi-tiered model. In J. K. Klingner, J. J. Hoover, & L. Baca (Eds.), *Why do English language learners struggle with reading: Language acquisition or learning disabilities?* (pp. 75–92). Thousand Oaks, CA: Corwin Press.

Hoover, J. J. (2009). *Differentiating learning differences from disabilities: Meeting diverse needs through multi-tiered response to intervention.* Boston: Pearson, Allyn, & Bacon.

Hoover, J. J., Baca, L. M., Love, E., & Saenz, L. P. (2008). *National perspective in implementing response to intervention: Research Report.* Boulder, CO. Author.

Hoover, J. J., Klingner, J., Baca, L. M., & Patton, J. M. (2008). *Methods for teaching culturally and linguistically diverse exceptional learners.* Columbus, OH: Pearson.

Hoover, J. J., & Mendez Barletta, L. (2008). Considerations when assessing ELLs for Special Education. In J. K. Klingner, J. J. Hoover, & L. Baca (Eds.), *English language learners who struggle with reading: Language acquisition or learning disabilities?* (pp. 93–108). Thousand Oaks, CA: Corwin Press.

Hoover, J. J., & Patton, J. R. (2008). Role of special educators in multi-tiered instructional programming. *Intervention in School and Clinic* (43), 195–202.

Hosp, M. K., Hosp, J. L., & Howell, K. W. (2007). *The ABCs of CBM: A practical guide to curriculum-based measurement.* New York: Guilford Press.

Individuals with Disabilities Education Act (IDEA) (2004). *Amendments of 2004.* Washington, DC.

Jimerson, S. R., Burns, M. K., & VanDerHeyden, A. M. (Eds.). (2007). *Handbook of response to intervention: The science and practice of assessment an intervention.* New York, NY: Springer.

Johnson, E., Mellard, D. F., Fuchs, D., & McKnight, M. A. (2006). *Responsiveness to intervention (RTI): How to do it.* Lawrence, KS: National Research Center on Learning Disabilities.

Kirk, S. A., Gallagher, J. J., & Anastasiow, N. J. (2006). *Educating exceptional children* (11th ed.). Boston: Houghton Mifflin.

Klingner, J. K., & Bianco, M. (2006). What is special about special education for culturally and linguistically diverse students with disabilities? In B. Cook & B. Schirmer (Eds.), *What is special about special education?* (p. 37–53). Austin, TX: PRO-ED.

Klingner, J. K., & Edwards, P. E. (2006). Cultural considerations with response to intervention models. *Reading Research Quarterly, 41* (1), 108–115.

Klingner, J., Hoover, J. J., & Baca, L. (Eds.). (2008). *Why do English language learners struggle with reading: Language acquisition or learning disabilities?* Thousand Oaks, CA: Corwin Press.

Klingner, J. K., Mendez Barletta, L. M., & Hoover, J. J. (2008). Response to intervention models and English language learners. In J. K. Klingner, J. J. Hoover, & L. Baca, (Eds.), *English language learners who struggle with reading: Language acquisition or learning disabilities?* (pp. 37–56). Thousand Oaks, CA: Corwin Press.

Klingner, J. K., Sorrells, A. M., & Barrera, M. T. (2007). Considerations when implementing response to intervention with culturally and linguistically diverse students. In D. Haager, J. Klingner, & S. Vaughn (Eds.), *Evidence-based reading practices for response to intervention* (pp. 223–244). Baltimore, MD: Brookes Publishing.

Marston, D., Reschly, A. L., Lau, M. Y., Muyskens, P., & Canter, A. (2007). Historical perspectives and current trends in problem solving: The Minnesota story. In D. Haager, J. Klingner, & S. Vaughn (Eds.), *Evidence-based reading practices for response to intervention* (pp. 265–285). Baltimore, MD: Brookes Publishing.

Mason, J. L. (1993). *Cultural Competence Self Assessment Questionnaire.* Portland, OR: Portland State University—Multicultural Initiative Project.

McCook, J. E. (2006). *The RTI guidebook: Developing and implementing a model in your schools.* Horsham, PA: LRP Publications.

McMillan, J. H. (2001). *Essential assessment concepts for teachers and administrators.* Thousand Oaks, CA: Corwin Press.

Mellard, D. F., & Johnson, E. (2008). *RTI: A practitioner's guide to implementing response to intervention.* Thousand Oaks, CA: Corwin Press.

Moen, P., Elder, Jr., G. H., & Luscher, K. (1995). *Examining lives in context: Perspectives on the ecology of human development.* Washington, DC: American Psychological Association.

Moran, D. J., & Malott, R. W. (2004). *Evidenced-based educational methods.* Boston: Elsevier Academic Press.

National Association of State Directors of Special Education, Inc. (NASDSE). (2005). *Response to intervention: Policy considerations and implementation.* Alexandria, VA: Author.

National Center for Culturally Responsive Teaching (NCCRESt) Position Statement. (2005). *Cultural considerations and challenges in response to intervention models* (Author). Retrieved February 1, 2008, from http://www.nccrest.org.

National Research Council (NRC). (2002). *Scientific research in education.* Washington, DC: National Academies Press.

No Child Left Behind Act. (2001). The Elementary and Secondary Education Act of 2001, P.L. 107–110, 115, *Stat.1425.* Washington, DC.

O'Malley, J. M., & Pierce, L. V. (1996). *Authentic assessment for English language learners: Practical approaches for teachers.* Boston: Addison-Wesley Publishing.

O'Neill, R. E., Horner, R. H., Albin, R. W., Sprague, J. R., Storey, K., & Newton, J. S. (1997). *Functional assessment interview for problem behavior: A practical handbook* (2nd ed.). Pacific Grove, CA: Brooks/Cole.

Ortiz, A. A., Wilkinson, C. Y., Robertson-Courtney, P., & Kushner, M. I. (2006). Considerations in implementing intervention assistance teams to support English language learners. *Remedial and Special Education, 27* (1), 53–63.

Pierangelo, R., & Giuliani, G. (2006). *The special educator's comprehensive guide to 301 diagnostic tests.* San Francisco: Jossey-Bass.

Reschly, A. L., Coolong-Chaffin, M., Christenson, S. L., & Gutkin, T. (2007). Contextual influences and response to intervention: Critical issues and strategies. In S. R. Jimerson, M. K. Birns, & A. M. VanDerHeyen (Eds.), *Handbook of response to intervention: The science and practice of assessment and intervention* (pp. 148–160). New York: Springer.

Rhodes, W. C., & Tracy, J. L. (1978). *Emotionally disturbed and deviant children: New views and approaches.* Englewood Cliffs, NJ: Prentice-Hall.

Shapiro, E. S. (1996). *Academic skills problems: Direct assessment and intervention.* New York: Guilford.

Shapiro, E. S. (2008). Best practices in setting progress-monitoring goals for academic skill improvement. In A. Thomas & J. Grimes (Eds.), *Best practices in school psychology V,* (pp. 141–157). Bethesda, MD: National Association of School Psychologists.

Shinn, M. R. (1989). Identifying and defining academic problems: CBM screening and eligibility procedures. In M. R. Shinn (Ed.), *Curriculum based measurement: Assessing special children* (pp. 90–129). New York: Guilford.

Thompson, S. J. (2004). Choosing and using accommodations on assessments. *CEC Today, 10* (6), 12.

Vaughn, S. (2003). *How many tiers are needed for response to intervention to achieve acceptable prevention outcomes?* Paper presented at the National Center on Learning Disabilities Responsiveness-to-Interventions Symposium, Kansas City, MO. December, 2003.

Vaughn, S., & Fuchs, D. (2003). Redefining learning disabilities as inadequate response to instruction: The promise and potential problems. *Learning Disabilities: Research & Practice, 18* (3), 137–146.

Vaughn, S., Linan-Thompson, S., & Hickman, P. (2003). Response to instruction as a means of identifying students with reading/learning disabilities. *Exceptional Children, 69* (4), 391–409.

Wallace, G., & Hammill, D. D. (2002). *Comprehensive receptive and expressive vocabulary test: Examiner's Manual* (2nd ed.). Austin, TX: PRO-ED.

Webber, J., & Plotts, C. A. (2008). *Emotional and behavioral disorders: Theory and practice.* Boston: Allyn & Bacon.

Wiley, T. G. (1996). Literacy and language diversity in sociocultural contexts. *Literacy and language diversity in the United States.* Washington, DC: Center for Applied Linguistics and Delta Systems.

Wright, J. (2007). *RTI toolkit: A practical guide for schools.* Port Chester, NY: Dude Publishing.

Ysseldyke, J. E., & Christenson, S. L. (2002). *FAAB: Functional assessment of academic behavior: Creating successful learning environments.* Longmont, CO: Sopris West.

Index

187

DATE DUE

MAR 2 9 2010

Demco, Inc. 38-293

CORW

A SAGE Compa

The Corwin logo—a raven striding across an open book—represents the union of courage and learning. Corwin is committed to improving education for all learners by publishing books and other professional development resources for those serving the field of PreK–12 education. By providing practical, hands-on materials, Corwin continues to carry out the promise of its motto: **"Helping Educators Do Their Work Better."**